the Writer's Craft

Valerie Thornton

Hodder Gibson

A MEMBER OF THE HODDER HEADLINE GROUP

The Publishers would like to thank the following for permission to reproduce copyright material:

Picture credits

p.3 © Turbo/zefa/Corbis; p.14 © H. Benser/zefa/Corbis; p.25 Stephen Johnson/Stone/Getty Images; p.37 PurestockX; p.52 © f1 online/Alamy.
All other photographs © Valerie Thornton

Acknowledgements

'The Ungrateful Queen' (extract) © Joanne Deans; 'Red Bird' © Valerie Thornton; 'Getting Sent For' (extract) © Donald Hutton; 'Thowar Boway' (extract) © Stuart McLardie; 'Determination', copyright Richard McQuarrie, from Discoveries, The Pushkin Prizes in Scotland, 2003; 'Answer Me' (extract) © Sarah Reynolds; 'The Meteor Shower' © Valerie Thornton; 'The Challenge', copyright Rebecca Low, from Going Places, The Pushkin Prizes in Scotland, 2004; 'A Midwinter Night's Dream', copyright Margaret Walker, from Going Places, The Pushkin Prizes in Scotland, 2004; 'The Magpie's Secret' (extract) © Kathleen Daly; 'Looking After Your Bicycle' © Valerie Thornton; 'The Snake's Wishes' © Rachael Cassidy; 'My Last Day at School' © Michael Chromy; 'Jacob's Chicken' by Miloš Macourek. Reprinted from *Prairie Schooner*, Volume 66, number 4 (winter 1992) by permission of the University of Nebraska Press. Copyright 1992 by the University of Nebraska Press; 'Sequel to Jacob's Chicken' © Marilyn Copland; 'An Ignorance of Sound' © Lesley Sargent; 'Two Wee Mice' by Carolyn Mack is reproduced by permission of Polygon, an imprint of Berlinn Ltd; 'The Myths of Childhood Uncovered' and 'My One True Friend' © Laura J. Rennie; 'No More Birthdays' and 'Deformed Finger' from MOTHER SAID by Hal Sirowitz, copyright © 1996 by Hal Sirowitz. Used by permission of Crown Publishers, a division of Random House, Inc.; 'I Hate My Brother' © Owen Smith; 'Annual' © Jim C. Wilson; 'The Songs of Fish' © Gordon Meade. This poem also appears in the collection THE SCRIMSHAW SAILOR (published in 1996 by Chapman); 'The Hawk', from The Collected Poems of George Mackay Brown. Reproduced by permission of John Murray (Publishers); 'Castle O Burrian' © Yvonne Gray; 'Voices O Quendale Bay' © Christine De Luca. Every effort has been made to trace all copyright holders, but if any have been inadvertently overlooked the Publishers will be pleased to make the necessary arrangements at the first opportunity.

Although every effort has been made to ensure that website addresses are correct at time of going to press, Hodder Gibson cannot be held responsible for the content of any website mentioned in this book. It is sometimes possible to find a relocated web page by typing in the address of the home page for a website in the URL window of your browser.

Papers used in this book are natural, renewable and recyclable products. They are made from wood grown in sustainable forests. The logging and manufacturing processes conform to the environmental regulations of the country of origin.

Orders: please contact Bookpoint Ltd, 130 Milton Park, Abingdon, Oxon OX14 4SB. Telephone: (44) 01235 827720. Fax: (44) 01235 400454. Lines are open from 9.00 – 5.00, Monday to Saturday, with a 24-hour message answering service. Visit our website at www.hoddereducation.co.uk. Hodder Gibson can be contacted direct on: Tel: 0141 848 1609; Fax: 0141 889 6315; email: hoddergibson@hodder.co.uk

© Valerie Thornton 2006
The moral right of Valerie Thornton to be identified as the Author of this Work has been asserted by her in accordance with the Copyright, Designs and Patents Act 1988.
First published in 2006 by
Hodder Gibson, a member of the Hodder Headline Group
2a Christie Street
Paisley PA1 1NB

Impression number   10 9 8 7 6 5 4 3
Year   2010 2009 2008 2007

Cover photo Top: plainpicture GmbH & Co. KG/Alamy; Bottom left: Hisham Ibrahim/Photov.com/Alamy; Bottom right: Stockbyte Platinum/Alamy
Typeset in 11/14pt Stone Serif by Phoenix Photosetting, Chatham, Kent
Printed and bound in Great Britain by Martins The Printers, Berwick-upon-Tweed

A catalogue record for this title is available from the British Library

ISBN-13: 978-0-340-91371-0

CONTENTS

Part One The Writer's Toolkit

Part Two Writer's Craft Assessment Tasks

CONTENTS continued

The Writer's Toolkit

Introduction: Knowledge About Language

You are lucky to be working with English! It is a very rich and beautiful language with origins that go back hundreds and thousands of years and with words that come from many different parts of the world.

Have you ever thought about where our words come from? Here are a few examples for you: 'whisky' comes from the Gaelic for 'water of life', 'omelette' is a French word, 'bungalow' is a Hindi word from India, 'pasta' is an Italian word, 'igloo' is an Inuit word from Greenland and northern Alaska, 'rucksack' is a German word, 'moccasin' is a Native American word and finally, 'bicycle' is unusual in that the first half of the word comes from the Latin for 'two' and the second half from a Greek word meaning 'circle' or 'wheel'.

Can you guess, or find out from a good etymological dictionary (one that gives you the *origin* of the word as well as its meaning) where the following words come from?

★ kalashnikov	★ pyjamas	★ onomatopoeia
★ piano	★ kaleidoscope	★ skirt
★ koala	★ magazine	★ yacht
★ shoogle	★ voodoo	★ skunk
★ restaurant	★ khaki	★ kiwi

English is a complex language which can lead to the extremely precise use of words and which allows you enormous fun crafting words and the ideas that they give life to. It is constantly changing, with new words being added, or old words being used in new ways. An example of a word that has changed its meaning over the years is 'silly'. Several hundred years ago, 'silly' meant only simple and uncomplicated, not stupid.

The arrival of the Internet has increased our vocabulary. We have new words such as 'e-mail', 'blogging' and 'phishing'. Can you see how these three words connect in meaning to, but are different from, words we already use? The words 'mouse', 'surf' and 'spam' have gained new meanings. Can you see any connection between the old and the new meanings of these three words?

Can you think of any words that we may not need now, but that we needed 50 years ago, before the use of computers became widespread? In the same way as our lives and lifestyles are

constantly changing, so our language is constantly adapting to fit our needs.

We use language without even thinking about it. When we talk or write, we are not usually aware of which parts of speech we are using, nor how we construct our sentences. However, if we become aware of the grammatical structures and the mechanisms that make our language work, then we can appreciate the writing of others and write better ourselves.

This part of this book is in three sections. The first section revises and explains **parts of speech**, which are labels to help us classify words according to what they do.

The second section looks at how we use these parts of speech in groups of words called **phrases** or **clauses** to say what we mean.

The third section explores how we can use these tools and other literary techniques to craft our masterpieces.

Parts of Speech

Nouns and Pronouns

All **nouns** are naming words – 'frog', 'car', 'apple', 'house'. Some nouns have capital letters and are called **proper nouns** because they are the name of a person, a place or day or month – 'Thomas', 'Benbecula', 'Wednesday', 'April'.

Some nouns which represent a living thing or object, which are 'pro' or 'on behalf of' that thing, are called **pronouns**. They include the following **personal pronouns**: 'I'/'me', 'you', 'he'/'him', 'she'/'her', 'it', 'we'/'us' and 'they'/'them'. For example, instead of saying 'Thomas is coming from Benbecula. Thomas'll arrive on Wednesday,' we use a personal pronoun in place of 'Thomas' the second time – 'Thomas is coming from Benbecula. He'll arrive on Wednesday.' We need pronouns to avoid constant repetition of nouns.

Other pronouns include: 'myself'/'yourself', 'mine'/'yours', 'someone'/'anyone'/'no-one'. Can you do the following exercise and fill in the rest of the pronouns?

Exercise

 Pronouns

Complete the following table:

I	myself	mine
you (singular)	yourself	yours
he		
she		
it		
we		
you (plural)		
they		

We also have concrete and abstract nouns. A **concrete noun** is something definite, something you can see or confirm with any of your five senses – for example, 'book', 'shouting', 'scent', 'sweetness', 'warmth'.

An **abstract noun** defines something you can't see, hear, smell, taste or feel – for example, 'eternity', 'thought', 'hope', 'time'. Writers, and especially poets, can come up with good ideas when they *do* try to define abstract nouns in concrete terms – for example, the colour of hope, the taste of loneliness, the sound of silence, the shape of happiness.

Most writers use mainly concrete nouns in their stories or poems, but often, the **theme** of their writing (the idea behind it), is an abstract noun. So, for example, while the **subject** of Laura J. Rennie's autobiographical piece, 'My One True Friend' (page 121) is her dog, Tessa, the themes are love and loss, which are abstract nouns. George Mackay Brown's poem, 'The Hawk', (page 149) is on the subject of a hawk (a concrete noun), but can you work out the themes, that is, the *ideas behind* the poem, that can be expressed as abstract nouns?

Sometimes a writer will decide to write about a specific subject, such as a person or a place. Both of these subjects are concrete nouns. Other writers decide to start with a theme, such as anger or injustice, which are abstract nouns, and to illustrate this with characters and situations. 'Jacob's Chicken', the short story by Miloš Macourek (page 92) is an example of the latter. (His name is pronounced **Mill**osh **Mat**so-reck.)

Mostly you are asked to write about specific subjects rather than to illustrate themes because themes are more complicated. However, you too can consciously use either of these two approaches. Your writing will be stronger if you are more aware of what you are doing.

Exercise

 ## Abstract and concrete nouns

This is an exercise to stretch your imaginative muscles. There are no right or wrong answers here. There may be no answers at all...

1 What colour would be a good colour for 'hope'?

2 What could 'loneliness' taste like?

3 What could 'silence' sound like?

4 What shape could 'happiness' be?

Use your five senses and see if you can find concrete expressions for the following abstract nouns: 'pain', 'time', 'anger', 'peace', 'hesitation', 'memory'.

Exercise

 ## Subject and theme

You will find it easier to understand subject and theme if you compare the different ways several writers here have used either the same subject or the same theme.

Here is a list of subjects or themes and the masterpieces in which you will find them. How does each writer use them in their own way?

1 Subject: **birds**
   'Jacob's Chicken' (page 92), 'Annual' (page 138),
   'The Hawk' (page 149), 'Castle O Burrian' (page 153)
   and 'Voices O Quendale Bay' (page 157).

2 Subject: **parent–child relationship**
   'My Last Day at School' (page 84), 'Two Wee Mice' (page 105),
   'The Myths of Childhood Uncovered' (page 115),
   'My One True Friend' (page 121), 'No More Birthdays' and
   'Deformed Finger' (page 128).

3 Subject: **teacher–pupil relationship**
   'My Last Day at School' (page 84) and 'Jacob's Chicken'
   (page 92).

4 Subject: **predator and prey**
   'My Last Day at School' (page 84), 'The Hawk' (page 149)
   and 'Castle O Burrian' (page 153).

5 Subject: **the natural world**
   'An Ignorance of Sound' (page 100), 'Annual' (page 138),
   'The Hawk' (page 149), 'Castle O Burrian' (page 153)
   and 'Voices O Quendale Bay' (page 157).

6 Subject: **magical creatures**
   'The Snake's Wishes' (page 79) and 'Jacob's Chicken' (page 92).

7 Theme: **conflict**
   'The Snake's Wishes' (page 79), 'My Last Day at School' (page 84),
   'Jacob's Chicken' (page 92), 'Two Wee Mice' (page 105),
   'The Hawk' (page 149) and 'Voices O Quendale Bay' (page 157).

8 Theme: **sound**
   'An Ignorance of Sound' (page 100), 'Annual' (page 138)
   and 'The Songs of Fish' (page 145).

9 Theme: **death**
'My Last Day at School' (page 84), 'Two Wee Mice' (page 105),
'My One True Friend' (page 121), 'No More Birthdays' (page
128) and The Hawk (page 149).

10 Theme: **fantasy**
'The Snake's Wishes' (page 79), 'My Last Day at School' (page 84),
'Jacob's Chicken' (page 92), 'An Ignorance of Sound' (page 100)
and 'The Myths of Childhood Uncovered' (page 115).

Have you noticed any other subjects or themes common to more
than one masterpiece?

Adjectives

Adjectives are words which describe nouns – a *sleepy* frog, a *new*
bike, a *mouldy* apple, a *gingerbread* house.

We need nouns to name objects (and ideas) but adjectives have
enormous power to describe those objects. For example, adjectives
can transform a 'pen' into a red gel pen, a broken ballpoint pen, a
gold fountain pen or even a sheep pen.

Think carefully about your choice of words, both nouns and
adjectives. Try to be as precise as possible. For example, the mouldy
apple above is a bit vague: 'the mouldy golden delicious' is more
precise and adds **assonance** (vowel rhyme), **alliteration** (deliberate
repetition of sounds for effect) and the **juxtaposition** (placing two
opposing ideas together for effect) of 'mouldy' and 'delicious'.

Can you explain, in grammatical terms, that is, in terms of nouns
and adjectives, what has happened to the word 'mobile' recently? It
used to be an adjective – describing which noun? What is it now,
and why has this happened? Can you also explain, in grammatical
terms, how the abbreviations 'CD', 'DVD' and the noun
'microwave' have arrived in our language?

> ### Fun With Words 1
>
> The Collie Dog
>
> A collie dog a melon saw
> and feeling rather jolly
> the collie ate the melon
> and then felt melancholy.
>
> The collie dog is in his grave
> the melon proved too sour
> and o'er his humble grave there grows
> a melancholy flower.

Verbs

Verbs are the parts of speech that give nouns the freedom to move, to do things. Without verbs, the sleepy frog, the new bike, the mouldy apple and the gingerbread house are static and silent. Bring in the verbs and suddenly the frog croaks, the bike skids, the mouldy apple flies through the air and the gingerbread house is eaten. Nouns and verbs are incomplete without each other.

Verb tense

Tense is about time and about how verbs can show past or present, and suggest future.

Most stories are written in either the **present tense** (right now) or the **past tense** (before now). Although stories can be *set* in the future, they still tend to be written in the present or past tense.

Here is an example of a story written in the present tense:

In the park, the wind is blowing all the leaves off the trees and so many leaves are lying on the ground that it is hard to tell where the path ends and the grass begins. A big black dog is racing through the leaves, kicking them up behind him. A woman wearing a red coat is running behind him waving and shouting at him to come back. Instead of going back to her, the dog suddenly stops and starts digging. Soon, he is prancing triumphantly around a large box he has uncovered...

You will notice that this story is happening now, today, right this minute, as we are reading it.

If it were instead written in the past tense, it would read like this:

In the park, the wind was blowing all the leaves off the trees and so many leaves were lying on the ground that it was hard to tell where the path ended and the grass began. A big dog was racing through the leaves, kicking them up behind him. A woman wearing a red coat was running behind him waving and shouting at him to come back. Instead of going back to her, the dog suddenly stopped and started digging. Soon, he was prancing triumphantly around a large box he had uncovered...

You will notice that this story has happened in the past, before now.

Can you think what the advantages and disadvantages are of writing a story in the present tense? Or in the past tense?

Here's how the story would sound if it were written in the future:

In the park, the wind will be blowing all the leaves off the trees and so many leaves will be lying on the ground that it will be hard to tell where the path ends and the grass begins. A big dog will be racing through the leaves, kicking them up behind him. A woman wearing a red coat will be running behind him waving and shouting at him to come back. Instead of going back to her, the dog will suddenly stop and start digging. Soon he will be prancing triumphantly around a large box he has uncovered...

You can see why we prefer to use present or past tense!

Let's see how other writers have used tense in this book. Look at the openings of the following pieces in this book and change, or try to change, the tense from past to present or vice versa. Say what impact this has on how well the writing works.

Look first at Yvonne Gray's poem, 'Castle O Burrian', (page 153) and see what happens if you change the tense.

Then try the same experiment with George Mackay Brown's poem, 'The Hawk' (page 149).

See what happens if you change the tense of 'My One True Friend' by Laura J. Rennie (page 121) and of 'A Midwinter Night's Dream' by Margaret Walker (page 73).

Now look at the start of Michael Chromy's short story, 'My Last Day At School' (page 84) and Rachael Cassidy's short story, 'The Snake's Wishes' (page 79). Why is it so difficult to change the tense of these two stories?

What conclusions can you draw about the need to choose the right tense?

Fun With Words 2

The Smellag Ass

The smellag ass ascends to pass
thro' crannies, nooks and manholes
but watch, begoad, for 'twill explode
if chased by lighted candholes.

(from a series on Domestic Pets, in the Glasgow University Magazine, *Ygorra*, in the 1930s)

Adverbs

Adverbs are words which describe a verb. They usually end in '–ly' – for example, the frog croaks *loudly*, the bike skids *dangerously*, the mouldy golden delicious flies *silently* through the air and the gingerbread house is eaten *greedily*.

Adverbs are good tools when they are used correctly. However, your writing will be more effective if you take the time to choose the best verb. In the first three examples in the previous paragraph, the verbs are strong verbs and the adverbs add meaning. The last example has a weaker verb. Can you think of a stronger, more precise verb we have that means 'to eat greedily'? The four adverbs above are fairly predictable ones. Can you think of any adverbs to replace them that are much more unusual, unexpected or even funny? Even changing around the adverbs above will produce startling results. Try it!

When you find yourself needing an adverb, make sure that you haven't overlooked a better verb. The best writers use very few adverbs. Have a quick look at any of the masterpieces in the third part of this book and see just how many adverbs you can spot.

You might also like to run a quick check on adjectives too, and see how different writers have different quantities of these two parts of speech that both add description.

Conjunctions and Prepositions

Two other parts of speech whose name and function you should know are *conjunction* and *preposition*. A **conjunction** is a connecting or joining word and enables you to link ideas. The most common conjunction is 'and', with 'but' and 'or' close behind.

A **preposition** is a word that gives you the position of an object – for example, the frog was *in* the pond, the bike was *on* the pavement, the mouldy golden delicious flew *through* the air and the gingerbread house was *below* a gingerbread tree.

Writer's Craft Toolkit Summary 1

You should now be familiar with the meaning and use of these writer's tools:

✓ **noun: pronoun, personal pronoun, proper noun, concrete noun, abstract noun**
✓ **adjective**
✓ **verb: present tense and past tense**
✓ **adverb**
✓ **conjunction**
✓ **preposition.**

II

More Helpful Tools and Construction Techniques

Word Analysis

Syllables are groups of letters that form units of sound. It is much easier to *hear* syllables, than to see them on the page. For example, 'can-did-ate' has three syllables, 'sil-ver' has two and all of these words have just one!

You can check the number of syllables by tapping your finger as you say the units of sound in any word. How many syllables are in the following words: 'television', 'enough', 'cough', 'examination'? Syllabic count is particularly important in some poetic forms. Look again at Jim C. Wilson's poem, 'Annual', (page 138), which is a series of haiku, and check that he has no more than 5–7–5 syllables in each three-line verse.

Think about how we speak English – do we give each syllable the same length and emphasis? What does it sound like if we do? We will return to this idea when we look at rhythm (page 23).

An awareness of syllables helps us to both construct and deconstruct words. Can you see how, in the previous sentence, one extra syllable here changes the meaning of 'construct' to its opposite: '*de*-construct'?

There are four other terms we use as tools to help us analyse words. They are the **root** or **stem** (think of plants) which both mean the starting point of any word in terms of its meaning. We then add **prefixes** before the root and **suffixes** after the root to refine the meaning of the word. For example, let's take the root 'struct', which comes from 'structum', which is the past participle of the Latin verb 'struere' meaning 'to build'.

We can add prefixes or suffixes to make the meaning very particular. For example, we can use prefixes:

> *con*-struct   *de-con*-struct   *re-con*-struct   *in*-struct

And suffixes:

> struct-*ure*   struct-*ur-al*   struct-*ure-less*

And both prefixes and suffixes:

> *con*-struct-*ion*   *in*-struct-*ion*   *de*-struct-*ion*   *re-con*-struct-*ion*

Exercise

 ## Roots, prefixes and suffixes

Below are three roots, planted on the page for you, so you can grow
your own words from them. See how many different prefixes and/or
suffixes you can add to each root. Use an etymological dictionary
(one with the origins of the meaning too) to help you if you wish.

1 'vis' from 'visum', the past tense of the Latin word 'videre'
  meaning 'to see'

2 'port' which is from the Latin word 'porta' meaning 'gate'

3 'plode' or 'plos', both of which come from the Latin verb
  'plaudere' meaning 'to clap your hands'. Can you think of an
  English word also from this Latin verb which means 'to clap
  your hands'? How do the words you can create from the root
  'plode' connect to the idea of clapping hands?

Here are three prefixes. See if you can fix them to several different
roots.

1 'tele–' which is the Greek word meaning 'far'

2 'trans–' which is a Latin preposition meaning 'across' or 'beyond'

3 'anti–' which is a Greek preposition meaning 'against'

Here are three suffixes – see what roots and/or prefixes you can
attach before them!

1 '–ing'

2 '–ate'

3 '–logy'

Look up the words you have made in an etymological dictionary and see whether they come from Latin or Greek or another language.

Finally, you should be familiar with vowels and consonants but just in case you need a reminder, **vowels** are the letters 'a', 'e', 'i', 'o', 'u' and **consonants** are every other letter. There are quite a few words that contain every vowel. The shortest word with all five vowels, only once each, and in the right order, is 'facetious'. (It's pronounced 'fa-**see**-shus', with the emphasis on the middle syllable, and means 'sarcastically humorous'.)

Punctuation

Punctuation consists of all the marks, other than actual letters, in a piece of text. These small marks are coded messages to you, the reader: they say things like 'here is the end of a sentence' or 'you should pause here' or 'someone is about to begin speaking' or 'this is the end of a question'.

You will have recognised the four punctuation marks referred to above as the **full stop**, the **comma**, **quotation marks** and the **question mark**. You should be very good at using them all by now. You should also be familiar with **brackets** and **exclamation marks**. The **ellipsis** (three dots '…') can also be useful. Its name comes from a Greek word that means 'to fall short' and we use it when something we are writing is unfinished or missing. It is *always* three dots – no more, no fewer.

There are three more punctuation marks that some writers are less confident about using. These are: the semi-colon, the colon and the apostrophe.

The **semicolon** (;) and the **colon** (:) are both used to create a break within a sentence. The semicolon is used between two similar clauses (a **clause** is a group of words containing a verb) within the same sentence – for example, 'The sun is shining; it is golden.' You can test for the correct use of a semicolon by replacing it with the word 'and'. Your sentence should still make sense.

The colon, which is a more powerful punctuation mark than the semicolon, is used to separate the first part of a sentence from a second part that changes, or builds on, the meaning of the first part – for example, 'He came home from school: he was brought home from school.' You can test for correct use of a colon by replacing it with the words 'or rather'.

A colon is also used to introduce quotes or a list.

Apostrophe

Apostrophes are tricky little things, but it is not difficult to learn how to use them correctly.

They have two separate uses. The first is to indicate **contractions** or a missing letter (or letters); the second is to indicate possession.

Examples of apostrophes that indicate contractions include:

★ she has → she's
★ they have → they've
★ I would → I'd
★ who is → who's
★ can not → can't
★ of the clock → o'clock
★ it is → it's.

Please note the *only* time 'it's' has an apostrophe is when it is short for 'it is'.

Can you give six other examples of words with apostrophes that indicate contractions? Also give, as above, the words in full before they have been contracted.

The **possessive apostrophe** followed by the letter 's' is used to indicate ownership by one *single* person – for example, 'Michael's guitar', 'Tracy's book', 'the cat's toys', 'the parrot's cage'.

You can confirm that a possessive apostrophe is correct by turning the phrase around to check that it is the guitar *that belongs to* Michael, the book *that belongs to* Tracy, the toys *that belong to* the cat, the cage *that belongs to* the parrot.

If the owner's name ends in an 's', then you still add "s' – for example, 'James's desk', 'Robert Burns's poems', 'the boss's office'.

If more than one person owns something, and the plural word doesn't end in 's', then again, you add "s' – for example, 'the women's handbags', 'the children's school', 'the men's tournament'.

However, most plurals do end in 's', and in these cases, the apostrophe goes *after* the 's' that indicates plurality. Generally, a second 's' is avoided because it makes pronunciation too cluttered – for example, 'the dogs' dishes', 'the caterpillars' chrysalises', 'the pigeons' food', 'the ships' anchors'.

Please remember that there are *never* any apostrophes with the following possessive pronouns: 'its', 'his', 'hers', 'ours', 'yours', 'theirs'. Most people would never dream of putting an apostrophe in the last five words on that list, but the first one causes lots of confusion.

You simply have to remember that 'its', when used possessively, is like 'his' or 'hers' and never has an apostrophe – so, for example, 'the dog wagged its (or his) tail', 'the cat licked its (or her) paw', 'the storm ran its course'.

Exercise

 ## Apostrophes

Here are seven testing sentences for you to correct by adding apostrophes in the right places.

1 Marks dinner was so cold that he couldnt eat it.
2 I havent got a clue where Maries pen is.
3 Its on the teachers desk.
4 The childrens jotters arent on that shelf.
5 Although its not easy, Peters hopes are high.
6 The lions trainer opened its mouth very carefully.
7 The lions trainer opened their mouths very carefully.

Now look again at each sentence and note whether each apostrophe you've added is indicating possession or contraction.

Fun With Words 3

The Allotment Love Letter

I am so melon-cauli dear
Since you have bean away
The thyme has seemed so very long
I pine for you each day.
No sugar beets your sweetness
Don't turnip your nose at me
But take this 18 carrot ring
And lettuce married be.
PS Allotment but not very mushroom.

Grammatical Analysis

The following section is a very brief introduction to the way we talk about the structure of our language. This is a fascinating area that can be studied in its own right at university level.

Much of the following section is quite challenging if you're unfamiliar with the terms we use for grammatical analysis. However, if you take it slowly, it should become clear.

Sentences

A **sentence** is a unit of sense. It begins with a capital letter and ends with a full stop.

We have already learned (or revised) the names for individual parts of speech such as nouns, verbs and adjectives but there are also terms to explain how these all work together in groups of words within sentences to make sense.

For example, one of the simplest sentences is 'Seals swim.' It is a complete unit of sense, containing one noun and one verb. Neither word would make much sense without the other.

We can also talk about this (and every other) sentence in terms of its **structure** – that is, how words are grouped together to make meaning happen.

Two very helpful words are **subject** and **predicate**. The subject is a noun, or a phrase containing a noun, that relates to the verb. The grammatical word for this relationship is **agreement**. The predicate is everything else, including the verb.

> Seals/swim.
> subject/predicate

You may have noticed that sentences aren't always so simple! But they will still have a subject and a predicate.

> Lots of Atlantic seals/swim in our coastal waters.
> subject/predicate

Here's how to work out the subject. First, find the main verb (sometimes the sentence has more than one verb). For example, the main verb above is 'swim'. Then ask yourself 'what swim?'. The answer to this 'what' question is the subject of the sentence, and in this case the subject is 'lots of Atlantic seals'. The rest of the sentence is the predicate.

You'll notice that our original sentence 'Seals swim.' is at the heart of this second sentence and that both the subject and the predicate have become a little bigger. The subject has expanded into a noun phrase and the predicate is now a clause that contains the verb and also a phrase giving us more information, which is called the **complement**.

See if you can find the main verb, then work out the subject and predicate in the following sentences. Note that the verb can be more than one word.

1 In our coastal waters, lots of Atlantic seals swim.
2 Kingfishers are nesting on the river bank.
3 I see salmon in the river again.
4 We want to see them.
5 I'm going to the swimming pool tonight.
6 Are you going to the pool too?

Analysing sentence structure is quite complicated but when you begin to realise how it all works, it will feel good!

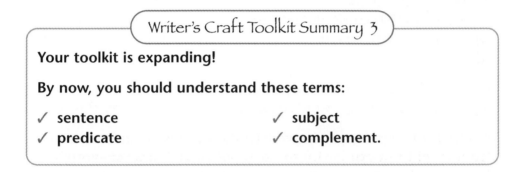

Writer's Craft Toolkit Summary 3

Your toolkit is expanding!

By now, you should understand these terms:

✓ sentence   ✓ subject
✓ predicate   ✓ complement.

Section III gives you some ideas about how to use these language tools to their best effect.

III

Literary Techniques for Crafting Your Writing into Masterpieces

Now that we have learned about (or revised) the raw materials for the craft of writing, we can look at some of the specialist techniques and concepts that we can employ to help us make the best use of these raw materials. In the same way as a master craftsman would take coloured ink and gold leaf and gild the pages of a book with his specialist tools, such as brushes and burnishers, we can now take nouns and adjectives, verbs and tenses, and burnish them with the literary tools in this section, into our own gilded masterpieces.

Do you know what a masterpiece is? Earlier on in this book (page 2), we were looking at how words change their meaning over the years.

Hundreds of years ago, there were Guilds of Master Craftsmen who were skilled in working with wood, stone, metal, leather, cloth, dyes and many more materials necessary in any society. In order to become a master, first you had to be an *apprentice* to a master. This meant that a master craftsman would agree to take you on as an apprentice and teach you all he knew. It used to take seven years.

When your apprenticeship was completed, you were then called a *journeyman* (because you had completed your seven-year journey through an apprenticeship). Before a journeyman could be elevated to the rank of Master, he would produce the best possible piece of work of which he was capable. He would then submit this, his *masterpiece*, to the Guild of Master Craftsmen to see if they thought he was good enough to join them. This was the original meaning of the word.

So, long ago, a masterpiece was like the present-day equivalent of a trial for a football team or an audition for a singing, dancing or acting part.

Now, we think of a masterpiece as the best work by someone who is already very good at what they are doing. Let's understand the word in *both* senses here and hope that in the production of the first kind

of masterpiece, we also work our way towards the second kind of masterpiece.

Here are some of the techniques used by those who are masterly at crafting with words.

Simile and Metaphor

Both **simile** and **metaphor** are figures of speech by which we compare things.

A simile always uses the words 'like' or 'as' to make the comparison, – for example, 'the corncrake flew *like* a haggis with wings' or 'the corncrake flew *as* clumsily *as* a haggis with wings'.

A simile keeps the object that is being compared *separate* from what it is being compared to.

A metaphor says one thing actually *is* another thing: the object being compared *becomes* what it's being compared to – for example, 'the corncrake *is* a haggis with wings'.

When we use metaphors, we are saying something that isn't true: the corncrake *isn't* a haggis. But metaphors get their power from making such dramatic connections!

As you can see from these examples, similes can be compressed into metaphors, and metaphors can be expanded into similes. Similarly, in the physical world, coal, which is carbon, can be compressed into diamonds. However, whether we could, or would ever want to, expand diamonds back into coal remains uncertain.

Both simile and metaphor are very useful tools for crafting your writing. Each has their place; metaphor is the more powerful.

If you need help to remember which is which, remember that the letters 's' and 'l' can be found in the three words 'simile', 'like' and 'as'. 'Metaphor' has neither of these letters.

For an excellent example of the contrasting effect of simile and metaphor, compare the poems by Heather Ann McTaggart and Owen Smith (pages 134 and 135).

Literal and metaphorical language

When we use language **literally**, we are saying something true – for example, 'I have six pieces of homework to do tonight.'

But if instead you complain, 'I've got tons of homework to do tonight!' then you are speaking **metaphorically**, and it couldn't be true. If you were speaking literally, you would need an articulated lorry to transport your homework about! But 'tons of homework' is a powerful metaphor (although it's a bit clichéd now) that gets over the idea of having a lot of homework.

We use metaphor, and exaggeration, quite a lot in English without even being aware of it. For example, we talk about couch potatoes, daybreak, and a mind that is racing. Can you think of any other examples of speaking metaphorically?

Exercise

 ### Simile, metaphor, literal and metaphorical language

Here are some examples of simile and metaphor. Can you say which is which?

1 The stonemason's hammer rang on the granite like gunshots.
2 The weaver's basketwork was as delicate as a wren's nest.
3 The goldsmith crafted a necklace of golden dreams.
4 On his first day, the young apprentice was a blank page.
5 The ropemaker's hawsers were as sinuous as cobras.
6 The fletcher's silver arrows were lightning in the air.

The following sentences are ambiguous because you don't have enough information to be sure whether the speaker is being literal or metaphorical. Explain what each sentence could really mean and what the situation might be, if it were (a) literal and (b) metaphorical.

1 I'm freezing to death.
2 I'm telling you, that spider was the size of a dinner plate!
3 I'm melting.
4 She is over the moon.
5 My dinner's frozen.
6 There were mountains of mashed potatoes.
7 I'm dying to get new trainers.

Metaphor and Abstract Nouns

In addition to using metaphor as a figure of speech, we also use metaphor to help us make the concepts (or ideas) behind abstract nouns more real. For example, we can think of opportunity, which is an abstract noun (see page 5), as a *window* through which we can see possibilities. Or, when we talk about the years rolling by, we are speaking metaphorically by using a *wheel* metaphor for time.

English is a very metaphorical language and very often we are unaware of this. But when our hearts sink, when our spirits rise, when we have butterflies in our stomachs or pins and needles in our arms, we are speaking metaphorically.

Can you work out which abstract nouns the first three of those four metaphors in the previous paragraph relate to? Can you think of any other metaphorical expressions?

Onomatopoeia

Can you remember which language the word 'onomatopoeia' comes from? (See page 2.) **Onomatopoeia** is when a word *sounds* like its meaning – for example, 'buzz', 'click', 'hiss', 'thump', 'slither'. Can you think of any other examples of onomatopoeia?

The highest number of examples of onomatopoeia in this book is in Gordon Meade's poem, 'The Songs of Fish' (page 145). How many can you find? Prose writers also use onomatopoeia, although not to the same extent.

Alliteration

Alliteration is the repetition of the same sound (not necessarily the same letters) at the beginnings of two or more words – for example, 'the cat lapped a carton of cream in the kitchen'. See if you can find two examples of alliteration in Jim C. Wilson's poem and in Yvonne Gray's poem (pages 138 and 153).

Rhythm and Rhyme

Like onomatopoeia and alliteration, rhythm and rhyme are ways of making patterns with sound.

We first touched upon rhythm when we revised syllables (page 12). We considered whether we give each spoken syllable the same amount of time and emphasis. If we did, our language would have a very monotonous rhythm, like a voice synthesiser or a Dalek.

Instead, we stress some syllables and not others. This gives our speech much more interesting rhythms, and also makes it easier to understand. Writers can use rhythm deliberately, in both poetry or prose, to make their writing more effective and entertaining. We can also *see* a rhythm on the page. Look at George Mackay Brown's poem (page 149) and Jim C. Wilson's poem (page 138) to see the visual rhythm they have created for the eye. Can you think of any other rhythms or visual patterns, moving or static, that you can see in the world around you?

Closely connected to rhythm is how long we take to pronounce a vowel. Normally we never think about this, but if, as a writer, you become aware of it, then you can use it to your advantage. In the following words, the vowels are **short vowels** and we say these quickly: 'cat', 'hit', 'pot', 'but', 'bet'. In this next group of words, the vowels are **long vowels** and we take more time to say them: 'weep', 'song', 'pool', 'blow', 'fine'. At the beginning of her story, 'The Snake's Wishes' (page 79), Rachael Cassidy uses words with long vowels. Think about what she is saying, and think about why the effect created by the long vowels is so appropriate.

Look at the following two lines from George Mackay Brown's poem, 'The Hawk' (page 149): '...and the blackbird/laid by his little flute for the last time.' Comment on the effects of his deliberate use of long and short vowels. Comment also on the effectiveness of vowel length in the last line of this poem.

Rhyme is found mostly in poetry or song and is again about sound. Rhyme is when two words have the same sound at the end of them – for example, 'lift/shift', 'bark/dark', 'shattered/mattered', 'today/betray'. Many modern poets prefer not to use full rhyme because they feel that it can distract the reader from the meaning.

Instead, they will disguise their rhymes a little with the following techniques. The first is **half rhyme**, where the consonant sound remains the same but the vowel sound is different – for example, 'sing/song', 'silver/salver', 'ripped/wrapped', 'moon/moan'.

The second is **assonance**, where the vowel sounds remain the same but the consonants change – for example, 'sing/fill', 'rock/bought',

'flower/trowel', 'diet/brighter'. Look at Jim C. Wilson's poem (page 138) and see what examples of assonance you can find there.

Rhyme is often, but not always, found at the end of a line of verse. Sometimes, it can be hidden *within* lines, when it is called **internal rhyme**. Can you find two examples of internal rhyme in Yvonne Gray's poem (page 153)?

Did you know that rhyme can also be masculine or feminine? If rhyme is on one syllable only, it's called masculine, for example, 'bring/wing', 'lot/taught', 'cash/dash', 'shout/out'.

If rhyme is on more than one syllable, it's called feminine. Feminine rhymes are especially useful for humorous effect, for example, 'shiver/quiver', 'caring/wearing', 'bickering/flickering', 'glowering/flowering', 'hippopotamus/quite a lot of us'!

You can have lots of fun with sound as a writer! If you are writing songs, then sound and singability and long vowels can sometimes be more important than meaning.

Personification

Not only do we use metaphor to say that things are what they aren't, but we also use **personification** to make things human that are not human. So for example, when we say that the table is *groaning* with food, we don't mean this literally – instead, we are talking about the table as if it were a *person* groaning under the weight of the food. See if you can find examples of personification in Jim C. Wilson's poem (page 138) and say what effect you think they have. Can you also find examples of personification in Yvonne Gray's poem (page 153) and in Rachael Cassidy's story (page 79)?

Symbolism

Symbols are very powerful things. An object or an image becomes a symbol when it also represents something other than itself – for example, there is a wild plant with purple flowers that also symbolises Scotland. (See if you can find out how this flower connects to the Latin motto of Scotland, *nemo me impune lacessit.)* Can you think of any other symbols for Scotland? Can you think of anything that symbolises any other country?

We can also use symbols in our writing. For example, what could the chicken and the teacher, and Jacob himself, symbolise in Miloš Macourek's story, 'Jacob's Chicken' (page 92)? Also, what might marinara sauce symbolise in Hal Sirowitz's poem, 'No More Birthdays' (page 128)? And the snake in Rachael Cassidy's story (page 79)? And the gull at the end of Yvonne Gray's poem (page 153)?

> ### Writer's Craft Toolkit Summary 4
>
> **You should now be familiar with the meaning and use of these writer's tools:**
>
> ✓ **simile**
> ✓ **metaphor**
> ✓ **metaphorical use of language**
> ✓ **literal use of language**
> ✓ **onomatopoeia**
> ✓ **alliteration**
> ✓ **rhythm, short vowels, long vowels**
> ✓ **rhyme, half rhyme, assonance, internal rhyme**
> ✓ **personification**
> ✓ **symbolism.**

Word Choice and Pace

You always have choices! You can choose words with long vowels or short vowels, you can write long sentences or short sentences, long verses or short verses, long paragraphs or short paragraphs.

Compare the different effect of sentence and paragraph length in 'Jacob's Chicken' (page 92), with 'My Last Day at School' (page 84).

In the same way as long vowels slow a word down, so long sentences and long paragraphs or verses are likely to slow the pace of your writing. Conversely, short vowels, short sentences and short paragraphs or verses can speed up the action.

Most pieces of writing need a variation of pace, so a mixture of short sentences and longer sentences usually works best.

Another factor that affects the pace of your writing is how much detail you provide. If you spend a long time describing something, perhaps even using short sentences, the pace of your writing would still remain quite slow.

You can speed up the pace by missing out unnecessary bits of information or description. We are familiar with the term *flashback* from film and television, and we can use this in our writing too when we go back in time within our writing.

We can also flash forwards and, if we only move a very little bit forwards in time, rather than calling it a *flash forwards*, we call it a *jump cut*. There is an excellent example of this in Laura J. Rennie's writing (page 121) where you will also find a full explanation of it.

Purpose

You should always be aware of what you're trying to do whenever you write something – the **purpose** of your writing. Writing is communicating and if you think about who you are trying to communicate with and what effect you are trying to have on them, it will make your writing easier. Sometimes we write only for ourselves, perhaps a diary or a shopping list, but usually there will be an **audience** for you. It could be your teacher, your classmates, or the wider world. When Heather, Owen, Rachael, Joanne and Laura were writing in their schools, they never expected that their work would appear in this book. So try to keep in mind that there might be someone out there who wants to read and publish your writing!

Think also about how you are trying to affect your audience. Do you want to tell them about something or to inform them? Do you want to entertain them? Are you trying to make them feel emotions, like anger or sorrow? Are you trying to create music from the sounds and rhythms of language?

When you know what the *purpose* of your writing is, then you are in a stronger position to achieve it.

First, Second or Third Person Narration

As well as choosing whether to tell your story using the present or the past tense, you can also choose whether to tell it as if it happened to you ('one day, *I* decided to get a cat'), or as if it happened to someone else ('one day, *Andrew* decided to get a cat'), or as if it happened to the person actually reading your story ('one day, *you* decided to get a cat').

We call 'I' the **first person**, 'you' the **second person** and 'he/she/it' the **third person**. Most stories are told, or **narrated**, in either first or third person.

Here is an example of *first person* narration:

One day, I decided to get a cat. I went to the pet shop but they told me they didn't sell cats, only birds, rabbits or fish. The man said to try the Cat and Dog Home instead. So I went to the Cat and Dog Home and they had so many animals all looking for homes that I didn't know which to choose. Eventually, I decided on a small ginger cat with a friendly face.

First person narration is like writing a letter or talking directly to someone. If this story were instead narrated in the *third person*, here's how it would read:

One day, Andrew decided to get a cat. He went to the pet shop but they told him they didn't sell cats, only birds, rabbits or fish. The man said to try the Cat and Dog Home instead. So he went to the Cat and Dog Home and they had so many animals all looking for homes that he didn't know which to choose. Eventually, he decided on a small ginger cat with a friendly face.

With third person narration, you, the writer, are more separate from the story you're telling.

We don't often use *second person* narration but here is how our story would read if it were narrated in the second person:

One day, you decided to get a cat. You went to the pet shop but they told you they didn't sell cats, only birds, rabbits or fish. The man said to try the Cat and Dog Home instead. So you went to the Cat and Dog Home and they had so many animals all looking for homes that you didn't know which to choose. Eventually, you decided on a small ginger cat with a friendly face.

Do you think this works as well as first person or third person narration? Can you say why?

Look at the five short story masterpieces (pages 79–114). How many are written in the first person? See if you can think your way through the opening paragraphs of each first person narrative, changing first person to third person, that is, changing 'I' to 'she' or 'he'. What impact does this have on the writing?

Next time you find yourself about to write a story, stop and think about whether it would be better written in the first person or the third person.

Point of View

When you are writing a story, you often have a choice of **point of view**. This means that you can make your readers see the story through the eyes of whichever character you want. For example, Laura's autobiographical piece, 'The Myths of Childhood Uncovered' (page 115), is written in the first person, from her own point of view, because she wants us to understand what she experienced. But the piece could be rewritten from the point of view of Bud, her big brother, and this would change it completely because his attitude and behaviour are very different.

Ask yourself the question: whose story do I *really* want to tell? The answer will tell you what your point of view should be.

Sometimes you should think a little more and ask yourself the next question: would a different point of view make my writing more *original*?

Voice or Persona

Voice or **persona** is the identity you assume in your writing, as the best way to tell the story. 'Persona' is the Latin word for an actor's mask. Have you ever worn a mask? A mask is a powerful thing. What effect does it have on how you feel and behave? Can you think who might wear masks now? And why?

Writers will often consciously choose the best voice in which to tell their story. For example, in 'Two Wee Mice' by Carolyn Mack on page 105, she chooses to write in the first person, but it's not in her own autobiographical voice. Instead she adopts the *persona* of a wee girl who is playing a ball game against a wall. Carolyn *isn't* a wee girl, but she puts herself in that position – acts it, if you like. It's like putting on a mask, or a disguise.

Here is an example of another persona:

> When I arrived at the scene of the crime, I observed that a total of six persons had apprehended the suspect. The Mercedes vehicle, previously notified as stolen, had been involved in a road traffic accident.

Whose voice might this be? What elements of style (vocabulary, sentence length, tone) give you a clue?

And whose voice might this be?

> We all sat on him till the polis came. He'd smashed the car up. It was a Merc.

In what ways is the content similar to the first persona? How does the expression of it differ?

Both of these voices, or personae, are invented. This is what you as a writer can also do.

A mask allows you to become a different person whether you put it on literally, as an actor in ancient Rome, or metaphorically, as a writer today.

Try the following exercise to explore personae.

> Charlie, a pet parrot, has escaped from his cage in the living room. There are two others in the room: the owner, an elderly lady called Hilda, and her other pet, a large black tomcat called Merlin.

Write three sentences in the persona of each of these three characters, that is, pretend you *are* these characters and put on the mask of a parrot, an old lady and a tomcat. What would each of them be thinking? How differently would they each speak? Use the first person, the 'I' voice, each time. Choose consciously either present or past tense, whichever you think works best.

Tone

In the same way as your *tone of voice* reveals your own attitude, **tone** reveals attitude in writing. So for example, if we compare the two accounts of the accident above, the first has a formal, somewhat pompous tone whereas the second has an informal, chatty tone.

How would you describe the tone of Michael Chromy's story, 'My Last Day at School' (page 84) as compared to that in Carolyn Mack's story, 'Two Wee Mice' (page 105)?

Tone is something we're not usually consciously aware of, whether spoken or written, although it always has a subconscious impact. However, it is another tool that you can use consciously to improve your writing.

Writer's Craft Toolkit Summary 5

You should now be familiar with the meaning and use of these writer's tools:

- ✓ verse/sentence/paragraph length
- ✓ pace
- ✓ purpose, audience
- ✓ first, second or third person narration
- ✓ point of view
- ✓ voice or persona
- ✓ tone.

Genre

Genre is a French noun that we've imported. It means 'a type' or 'a kind' and we use it help to classify different *types* or *kinds* of writing. So, for example, fiction and non-fiction are two different genres (types) of writing.

There are many different genres of fictional writing. For example, novels, short stories, poetry and drama are all broad fictional genres. Within each of those, we have more specific genres. For example, we can have detective fiction, horror fiction, science fiction or romantic fiction. Can you think of any more fiction genres?

There are also several genres of non-fiction writing – for example, news reporting, biography, technical writing, medical writing. Can you think of any more non-fiction genres?

Sometimes writing can belong to more than one genre. For example, Carolyn Mack's short story, 'Two Wee Mice', page 105, also belongs to a genre called **dramatic monologue**. *Dialogue*, as you know, is where *two* people speak: *monologue* is where *one* person speaks. (Can you think of any other words beginning with the Greek prefix 'mono–' that include the idea of oneness, singularity or uniqueness? See 'monogram' page 131). This story could be performed, with the words exactly as they are, by one person on a stage for an audience. In other words, unlike 'Jacob's Chicken' (page 92), this story is already dramatised.

As with tone, genre is something of which we are not normally conscious. However, each genre has its own characteristics and its own distinctive qualities.

Some genres are more complex than others. For example, a fable works on two different levels. It seems to be a simple story, whose purpose is to entertain, but behind it, the main purpose is to teach you a lesson. For example, Aesop wrote many fables more than two and a half thousand years ago using animals and personification to teach us lessons.

The story of the hare and the tortoise is one of his fables in which a hare and a tortoise agree to a race to see who is faster. The arrogant hare is so certain that it is faster, that it lies down for a rest on the way. The tortoise plods steadily past the sleeping hare and wins the race before the hare has woken up. The moral of the story is that if you are talented, like the hare, but you don't apply yourself, you will fail; and also that, if you keep going steadily, like the tortoise, even though it is a struggle, you'll get there in the end.

There are two stories in this book, 'The Snake's Wishes' (page 79) and 'Jacob's Chicken' (page 92) which also work on more than one level.

Can you say which particular genres 'The Snake's Wishes' (page 79) and 'My One True Friend' (page 121) belong to? What are the characteristics of each piece that lead you to this conclusion?

Format

Genre and format are closely related. Where genre is the *kind* of writing, **format** is the way it is laid out on the page, in paragraphs, verses and lines. It is also how blank lines, indentation of paragraphs and white space is used. Different genres require different formats. How would you describe the format of poetry, of a novel, of a newspaper and of a playscript? Which would you say has the most white space on the page? Why? And the least? Why?

Sometimes we create formats in order to give ourselves boundaries. In the same way as physical boundaries and rules have been developed so that we can play different games like football, tennis or snooker, so writers will also create boundaries within which they can play with words and ideas.

For example, you can decide to write a short story that is only 50 or 100 words long. Or, a poem with only three lines and no more than 5–7–5 syllables in each line. Or a 14-line rhyming poem with 10 syllables in each line. Or a five-line humorous poem where lines 1, 2 and 5 rhyme with each other, and lines 3 and 4, which are shorter, also rhyme with each other. Do you know the names we give each of these three forms of poetry?

Register, Accent and Slang

Register is how we define the different styles of language we use in different situations. For example, if you were at a meeting with your headteacher in their office, you would probably use a different register from that which you would use in the playground with a friend. In each case, your register should be *appropriate* to your situation.

The register we use in our writing is determined by our audience. Perhaps the best-known register is standard English. This is the formal English used in education, newspapers, television news and a book like this – well, most of this book. Look again at 'Two Wee Mice' (page 105). This piece is written much less formally. Carolyn Mack has adopted a persona to narrate her story. Remembering that register is determined by situation and audience, where would you say Carolyn's character is, and to whom is she speaking?

The register of this story is Glaswegian **dialect** or **vernacular**. Christine De Luca's poem (page 157) is also in dialect – not Glaswegian, but that of the Shetland Isles. Dialect and vernacular both mean a form of language that is particular to a region or a community. Dialects have their own vocabulary and **syntax**. (Syntax means word order.)

Accent is about sound, about pronunciation and, like dialect, regional accents are particular to a region or a community. So, for example, you can speak with what an American would recognise as a Scottish accent. This might be, to the more familiar ear of a fellow Scot, an Orkney accent, an Aberdeenshire accent, a Western Isles accent or a Glaswegian accent.

Fun With Words 4

Un Petit d'un Petit

Un petit d'un petit
S'étonne aux Halles
Un petit d'un petit
Ah! Degrés te fallent
Indolent qui ne sort cesse
Indolent qui ne se mène
Qu'importe un petit d'un petit
Tout Gai de Reguennes

Luis D'Antin Van Rooten, from Mots d'Heures: Gosses, Rames

(If this seems incomprehensible, find someone who can read French aloud and *listen* carefully!)

Slang means words that are very informal, usually spoken rather than written and definitely not standard English. Slang is often used by younger people to say how good or how bad something is – for

example, 'cool' or 'wicked' or 'spiffing'. Slang goes out of fashion very quickly.

Most of the writing you do will be in standard English. But if you're writing stories you might want to write in dialect or to indicate accent. This can be almost as difficult as writing in another language because there are seldom standard spellings.

If you are trying to write in dialect or to indicate an accent, don't try to 'translate' every single word: a few key ones will give your audience enough clues to hear the voice.

Look carefully at the first paragraph of 'Two Wee Mice' (page 105). This story is written in Glaswegian dialect. Count how many words there are in this paragraph and make a note.

Now count how many words there are in standard English.

Now count how many words are standard English words but that are *spelt* differently so that we *pronounce* them with a Glasgow accent.

Now count how many words, if any, are dialect words that only a Glaswegian would understand.

In fact, Carolyn has used very few dialect words in this entire story. While Glaswegian dialect does have some unique words, Carolyn wants her story to communicate as widely as possible, while still keeping a Glasgow accent.

This is in contrast to Christine's poem, where she uses a significant number of unique Shetlandic dialect words. In the book where her poem first appeared, *Sounds & Voes*, she has also written a standard English version to help non-Shetlanders understand.

Irony

It is helpful to know what irony is because it can give your writing an extra edge and introduce humour too. Both words and situations can be ironic.

If someone is **speaking ironically**, then they often mean the opposite of what they actually say. For example, if you accidentally drop your dinner plate food-side-down on the carpet, and your mum says, 'Well done!', she means it ironically, or sarcastically, not literally.

An **ironic situation** is where something someone does in good faith becomes pointless. Here is an example of a plot which combines

two ironic situations. It is a classic short story called 'The Gift of the Magi' written more than a hundred years ago by O'Henry in which a young man and his wife are very poor. It is Christmas Eve. Her only valuable possession is her beautiful long hair while his only valuable possession is his grandfather's beautiful gold watch. Each wants to buy the other a Christmas present. Can you see what's going to happen that would be ironic?

Yes – she sells her hair and he sells his watch and each buys their present. His present to her is a set of jewelled combs for the long hair she no longer has and her present to him is a chain for the watch he no longer has. This is a perfect example of a doubly ironic situation.

Black humour

Black humour is when something that is essentially sad, shocking or painful is related in such a way that we end up laughing. Sick jokes often depend on black humour.

Here are two examples of recent news stories which are both ironic and blackly humorous.

> First, there was the Swedish hunter who was knocked out when a goose shot by his son fell on his head. Second, there was a rare American thrush that made it all the way across the Atlantic to land, exhausted, in Shetland, where it was promptly eaten by a cat!

Text Messaging

Text messaging, or 'texting', is a shorthand way of communicating in writing, usually by mobile phone or e-mail.

Longhand is the way we normally write. *Shorthand* was originally developed because we speak faster than we can write in longhand. In shorthand, words were reduced to lines and squiggles that could be written as quickly as we speak. It was used by secretaries and newspaper reporters in the years before tape recorders became small enough to be portable. Now, with high-quality, miniaturised recording equipment, and speech-to-text software, shorthand is no longer needed.

Think about text messaging. Why has it developed? What is the purpose of sending a message in 'txt'? (You might like to think about time and money!) What kinds of messages are sent by 'txt'? And what kinds of messages wouldn't be? Why not? What is the register of text messaging?

How would you explain to someone the rules of text messaging? Think about the relationship between sound and spelling. What features does it have in common with normal writing? How is it different? Think about the way that words are changed: would you say that vowels or consonants are more important? Why?

What do you think are the strengths of texting? And the weaknesses? Think about the vocabulary of text messaging: how big would a dictionary be for it? Why? See if you can come up with 20 entries for it.

Who exchanges text messages? Who doesn't? Is it intended to be a secret language, like Nushu, which is a 400-year-old Chinese language for women only? (The last fluent speaker of this language, Yang Huanji, has just died, in her nineties. Why do you think this language might have died out with her?)

Some teachers are complaining that pupils are introducing texting techniques into their formal schoolwork. Do you think it should be acceptable or not? Why? You might like to think about the difference in content and style between a message and an extended piece of writing.

Now try to 'translate' the previous paragraph into 'txt'!

What have you learned in the attempt?

Other methods of communication include Morse code and semaphore. See if you can find out why they were developed, and why we no longer need them. What do you think might replace texting?

Characterisation

Characterisation means creating characters. You can create **main characters** who star in your writing, and **minor characters** who have only brief walk-on parts. Think of a book, a film or television programme you have seen, and see if you can give examples of main characters and minor characters.

Before you begin writing, try to get to know your characters. Go for unusual details and use your senses. Ask yourself the following questions:

★ What does my character look like?

★ What do they wear?

★ How do they wear it?

★ What kinds of sounds do they make, their voices, their footsteps?

★ How do they smell, pleasant, unpleasant, artificial?

Make your answers unusual.

Here are three short but masterly descriptions of the visual appearance of three characters from the short story collection, 'Bad Dirt', by the American writer Annie Proulx (her surname rhymes with 'blue'):

> ... Kate, a blonde with a face she had clipped from a magazine and the caramel eyes of a lizard...

> ... Decker with his face like an arrowhead, eyes so pale a blue they looked turned inside out, and atop his lip a drizzly mustache.

(Both from *The American Wars Refought*)

> He was a tall man with heavy bones. His coarse skin
> seemed made of old leather upholstery, and instead of lips,
> a small seam opened and disclosed cement-colored teeth.

(From *What Kind of Furniture Would Jesus Pick?* Proulx chooses her titles carefully too.)

What impressions do you get of each of these characters, even from such brief descriptions? What kind of people are they? Look at how Proulx makes unusual comparisons, using both metaphor and simile, and at how effective the long vowels in the third description are, and at the way the idea of opened-and-closed is created. This is powerful and poetic writing: Proulx is playing as much with sound as image.

It is important to give your characters the right names. Names always come with associations, so make sure you want those associations. Can you think of any names that are associated with a young person, or an old person, or a particular nationality?

It also helps if you know what makes your character tick, what motivates them and if, instead of just describing them, you let them *do* something, then your writing will be more effective.

It helps too if you let them speak, if you use **dialogue** between characters. Dialogue is good because in addition to making your characters more alive, it also lets your characters relate to each other.

Look at the way the wee girl speaks at the beginning in 'Two Wee Mice' (page 105). Look at *what* she says, and also the *way* she says it. Compare this with how the mother is characterised, again by what she says and how she says it, in Hal Sirowitz's two poems (page 128).

If you're not sure how to lay out dialogue, have a look at Rachael Cassidy's story on page 79 of this book. Try to remember to take a new paragraph for each change of speaker and to put quotation marks at the beginning and end of each speech.

A Sense of Place

Giving a sense of place, or **setting the scene**, is how you indicate where a story or a poem is happening. Often, and in most of the

prose writing here in this book, a sense of place is not particularly important. In Miloš Macourek's story, 'Jacob's Chicken' (page 92), for example, we have a school, a garden and a zoo and how *exactly* each of these looks is not important in this story. Similarly, in 'The Snake's Wishes' (page 79), we have a town and a zoo, and again we don't need to know *exactly* what they're like.

Where it *does* matter, is when some aspect of the place is an essential part of the story. So, for example, in Miloš Macourek's story, the one important detail in the garden is 'the baby-blue currants' that Jacob's chicken eats. And in Rachael Cassidy's story, the one important detail about the town is that there are 'lots of poor people sitting in the street'.

Look at the description of the kitchen in the second paragraph of Michael Chromy's story, 'My Last Day at School' (page 84). Why is this essential to the story? Whom do these details characterise?

Look also at the description of the carpet in Laura J. Rennie's autobiographical piece, 'The Myths of Childhood Uncovered' (page 115). Why is this essential to her writing? Whom do these details characterise?

Sometimes a description of place is essential to the writing. Look at Jim C. Wilson's poem (page 138). What details does Jim give us of sights and sounds? How do they connect to the purpose of the poem?

Look at Yvonne Gray's poem (page 153). Again, a sense of place is essential here. What details does Yvonne give us? How do they connect to the purpose of the poem?

When the purpose of a piece of writing is to tell a story, the characters and the events tend to be more important (and to change and develop more) than the context. In such cases, it is the narrative, the **plot**, that is more important.

We often find a greater sense of place in poetry, because poetry is less about narrative, less about telling a story, and more about touching our senses and our emotions.

Sometimes, though, a writer will connect their characters closely to a place. For example, they might write about a lonely old sailor living in an old, leaky boat pulled up on the shore, or, they might include details of the weather, like a thunderstorm to accompany an argument between two people, then sunshine and a rainbow to symbolise when they make peace with each other again.

A sense of place is also important if you are trying to create atmosphere, particularly in ghost or horror stories. Here, the ruined house, the creaky door, the rattling window, the howling wind, the darkest of nights and those slow, heavy footsteps coming towards you up the echoing stairs are all powerful details of place that help you when your purpose is to terrify your reader.

By contrast, can you think of the kind of details of place that you could use to create a feeling of peacefulness in your reader? Think of a location, or a building, the landscape, the weather, the sounds, smells, the time of day and anything else that could add to the effect.

When you next write, think about how you could use a sense of place more in your writing to make a greater impact on your readers.

Plagiarism

Plagiarism is a deliberate and deceitful act of literary theft. If someone steals another writer's actual words and pretends they've written them themselves, then that is plagiarism.

If you find a phrase you like somewhere in this book and you copy it into a piece of your own, and pretend you wrote it, then that is plagiarism. If you copy one of the stories here and change a word here and a phrase or two there, and perhaps change the location and the names, and then pretend it's all your own work, that too is plagiarism. It is deliberate theft of another writer's work.

However, we all have to learn to write. And we learn by studying other writers. We learn to copy not their actual words, but their *ways* of writing.

In Part Two of this book, where you learn how to prepare for the Writer's Craft element in the National Assessment Bank, you are asked to analyse the way a writer is writing, and then to continue this writing by copying the writer's style and subject matter. This is *not* plagiarism because you are not pretending you've written the first part: if you did, then it would be plagiarism. But what this exercise does is help you learn to write better by practising writing in different styles. This will help you find your own voice and your own unique style.

> ## Writer's Craft Toolkit Summary 6
>
> **You should now be familiar with the meaning and use of these writer's tools:**
>
> ✓ **genre**
> ✓ **format**
> ✓ **register, dialect, vernacular, syntax, accent, slang**
> ✓ **text messaging**
> ✓ **characterisation, main character, minor character, dialogue**
> ✓ **place, setting the scene.**
>
> **You should also understand exactly what plagiarism is, and isn't.**

Structuring the Content

We have already looked at how words are 'con-struct-ed' from syllables, with roots, prefixes and suffixes. We have also looked at how sentences are constructed with subjects and predicates.

Now we are going to look at using sentences to construct paragraphs and entire stories. This is not unlike the way a master builder uses tools and raw materials to construct foundations, walls, windows, floors, ceilings and a roof – which then become a house. Purpose is very important here; you have to know whether you are creating a stone-built house for a family, or a wooden garage for a car, or a poem to make people happy, or a story to make people sad.

Look again at Michael Chromy's story (page 84). Look in particular at the very first paragraph. It is symmetrically structured so that he starts in the present, goes back millions of years and returns to the present. Can you identify the phrase that links the present to the past, and then the phrase that brings us back from the past to the present again?

Now look at the first sentence of each paragraph. Can you see how he has opened with a topic sentence that leads us into the subject of each paragraph?

Look again at Miloš Macourek's story (page 92). What do you notice about the way he has structured his sentences and paragraphs?

Now we are going to look at the structure of a whole piece of writing. Purpose is very important and will determine genre, register, tense, point of view and every other detail of the content.

So, for example, if you are writing a news story, the purpose is to inform your readers. The genre is non-fiction journalism, the register is formal, the tense is past tense, the point of view is third person. And the structure would be the same as for any news story which is that the most important and dramatic information is given first, followed by more details of decreasing importance. (If you are a tabloid journalist, no paragraph is more than one sentence long.) News stories have to be written so that paragraphs can be cut from the end by the newspaper editor without leaving the story appearing unfinished. Thus, the purpose determines the structure.

However, in this book we are looking mainly at creative writing, at fiction and poetry.

Unlike in news stories, endings in short stories and poems are essential and are often what the whole story or poem is working towards. Often too, they are structured so that there is a connection between the beginning (and the title) and the end.

Look again at Miloš Macourek's story (page 92) and Michael Chromy's story (page 84), this time thinking about the overall structure. They both have a very clear structure which hasn't happened by accident. How would you describe the structure of each?

Some writing is structured so that it is cyclical, that is, so that it comes back round to almost where it started. Look again at Jim C. Wilson's poem (page 138) and George Mackay Brown's poem (page 149) and see if you can see this structural pattern at work.

All writers plan their stories and poems; sometimes almost instinctively in their heads, sometimes very deliberately with lots of notes on lots of bits of paper.

Next time, before you begin writing, try to think about how you are going to structure your story. Most pieces of writing (and all the prose pieces and some of the poems here) are structured chronologically, with the content revealed in the order that it happens in time. This is a good guiding principle, particularly in shorter pieces of writing, but you still have the possibility of adding structural patterns, like connecting the beginning and/or the title with the end, or using flashbacks.

Planning a story

A story is a narrative in which something happens. Things *change* between the beginning and the end. As a writer, you have to come up with the ideas for events and changes. This is called the **plot**.

When we looked at creating a sense of place, we realised that although place is important too, plot is much more important. There are several concepts that can help you come up with a good plot.

The first is **conflict**. Conflict can be as direct as a fist fight between two people or as subtle as someone struggling with themselves about whether to steal something or not. For example, if we take Carolyn Mack's story (page 105) we can see that there are minor conflicts between the narrator and Mrs McCann, and between the 'big boays' and Sandy Paterson. But there are two major conflicts driving this story. First, the physically violent conflict between Mr Brady and his children, which then leads to the second conflict within John Brady himself who is torn between fear of his father's violence and his duty to save Danny. The tragic end of this story comes directly from this conflict in John Brady's head.

Think about any of the other short stories in the masterpiece section of this book and see if you can identify conflict, both minor and major.

The second concept that can help you come up with a good plot is **action**. Again, if we take Carolyn's story, there are several kinds of action which all add to the story. First, there is one action that gives the story its overall structure, which is the wee girl throwing her ball at a wall while singing songs and telling us the story. Second, within that, the narrator tells us about Mr Brady's actions, about the actions of all the adults out looking for Danny Williams, about what happened to her pencil and her da's dinner and her mother's rosary beads, and the biggest action of all down at the canal.

Think about any of the other short stories in the masterpiece section and see what action you can identify.

A third element that will make it easier for you to write stories well is if you can come up with *unusual characters*. Ordinary people doing ordinary things don't make great stories. But if you can create an unusual character (you can use aspects of real people for inspiration), then very often your unusual character will perform

unusual actions. If you then bring your unusual character into conflict with themselves or with another (unusual) character, if you give one or both of them a *problem*, then you will find your story much easier to write.

A fourth element is the **turning point**. Turning points are places in the narrative where there is a choice about the direction it could take. For example, in Carolyn's story, if John Brady's fear of his father hadn't been so great, he could have saved Danny's life.

Think about any of the other short stories in Part Three and see whether you can find any turning points.

Planning a poem

There are also several concepts that can help you write a poem.

The first is *purpose*. Short stories have a clear *narrative* purpose: they tell a story. Poems are a little bit different, because their main purpose is not to tell a story, but to make you see things differently, to help you hear the music of language, to share the fun the poet had patterning words and ideas, and to give you the pleasure or pain of original word pictures in your head.

Look again at any of the poems anywhere in this book and see if you can work out what the writer's purpose is.

Then, before you write your next poem, work out what your purpose is. What are you trying to achieve? For whom are you writing?

Second, although the structure of poems is very different from that of stories, it is still important. The solid block of texts from Hal Sirowitz are the right shape for the verbal and psychological thumping the mother is giving her child. Similarly, the delicate shape of Jim C. Wilson's poem on the page connects to the lightness and delicacy of his subject matter. Try to make sure that the shape of your poem on the page connects to the content.

Third, you have the music of language at your disposal. Try to use it! You have onomatopoeia, alliteration, assonance, vowel length, rhyme and rhythm.

Fourth, you have the magic wands of metaphor and simile to wave over your writing, to create spell-binding comparisons and images in your reader's mind.

Titles, Openings and Resolutions

Titles should be more than simply identification labels. For example, an obvious label-title for Carolyn Mack's story could be 'The Canal'; or 'Jacob's Chicken' could be called 'The Magic Picture'. Why are the writers' own carefully-chosen titles so much better than simple labels?

Try to think beyond an obvious label-title. Try to make all your titles connect more interestingly with your work. It can take some time to come up with the right title.

The opening of your story should also intrigue your reader enough to make them want to read on. It should create **suspense** by making us wonder where the story is going to go next.

Have a look at the openings of the short stories in either Part Two or Part Three of this book and see how they all work in different ways to create suspense and engage your interest. They raise questions such as: Who is this? What is happening? Why? What happens next?

The resolution of a piece of writing is not only the end, but is also a satisfactory conclusion. The questions raised at the beginning, or on the way through, should all have been answered and there should be a sense of completion and satisfaction.

Think about the resolution of the stories in Part Three. The best endings should always be both unexpected and yet inevitable. How successful are the endings here? Are they effective and satisfactory? What questions were raised earlier on, and how have they been answered and resolved? Try to make your own story endings as effective.

None of the examples in Part Two have either endings or resolutions because they are only beginnings. They are deliberately unfinished so that you can take them a little bit further. They are unresolved, unsatisfactory, incomplete.

In a poem, each and every word is important. Nonetheless, go for the best possible title, a good opening and an ending that develops from the ideas or images or techniques that you have used earlier.

Look at any of the poems anywhere in this book and see how successfully they begin and end.

> ## Writer's Craft Toolkit Summary 7
>
> **You should now be familiar with the meaning and use of these writer's tools:**
>
> ✓ **structure**
> ✓ **plot, narrative**
> ✓ **conflict, action, unusual characters, turning points**
> ✓ **title**
> ✓ **opening**
> ✓ **suspense**
> ✓ **resolution.**

Drafting and Redrafting

Very few writers produce perfect writing immediately. They will make notes, then first drafts, perhaps abandon that, make more notes, more drafts and finally end up with a piece of text they're reasonably happy with.

Here are some questions for you to answer before you start writing:

1 What is the purpose of this piece of writing?
2 Who are you writing for?
3 Can you make your idea more original?
4 Are your characters unusual in any way?
5 Is this best written in the first, second or third person?
6 Can you use any dialogue?
7 Is this best written in the present or past tense?
8 Can you connect the setting to the content?
9 Do you have any conflict or action?
10 What is the subject of your writing?
11 What is the theme?

When you've thought carefully about what you want to write, made notes and then made your first draft, you might not think it's perfect. This is where **redrafting** can help you.

In order to redraft successfully, you have to keep the purpose of your writing clear in your head. (Sometimes your purpose changes as you get a better idea and you might want to rewrite completely. This is a good sign and is part of the creative process.)

If you read over your first draft and feel that it's not working very well, that it's too short or you've got stuck, here are some questions you can ask yourself about your story or your poem.

1 Questions to help improve your short story:
- Is your plot sufficiently original?
- Are your characters sufficiently original and interesting?
- Could you be giving us more details about your characters or the setting?
- Do you need more conflict or action?
- Can you bring in another unusual character to make it work better?
- Can you use language more effectively perhaps with adjectives, alliteration, onomatopoeia, metaphor or simile?
- Could you use something as a symbol?
- Could you connect the beginning and the end?
- Have you come up with the best title?
- Have you read it aloud? (This is the best way to check for missing words, or unintentional repetitions, or bits that simply don't make proper sense.)

2 Questions to help improve your poem:
- Are your ideas sufficiently original?
- Will your reader now be able to see something with new eyes?
- Have you exploited the music of language, using techniques like onomatopoeia, alliteration, assonance, vowel length, rhythm and rhyme?
- Could your poem be improved with metaphors or similes?
- Does the shape look good on the page? (Make sure your lines are not too long!)
- Could you use something as a symbol?
- Have you come up with the best title?
- Have you read it aloud?

Copyediting

When you have done your best with the writing, the final stage is **copyediting**. This word comes from the publishing industry where text is referred to as 'copy'. A copyeditor is someone who takes a piece of copy and makes sure that technical details like spelling, punctuation and capitalisation are correct. They also make sure that the writer is consistent, for example, that a character's name is spelt the same way each time, and that the tense doesn't change unintentionally. A copyeditor helps a writer to make sure their writing is working as well as it possibly can.

Copyediting is completely separate from the creative process and, although you can do it yourself, it is often better if someone else copyedits your work. Why do you think this might be? (It's not unlike what your teachers do when they mark your stories or poems.)

Here are some guidelines to help you copyedit someone else's work, although you can also apply them to your own work. The first stage is to read for *sense*, the second is to *correct* the copy.

Reading for sense

Read the copy through carefully.

Does it make sense to you? If not, mark, highlight or make a note of the bits that are confusing and ask the writer to consider rewriting them. Sometimes a writer can be so close to a piece of writing that they don't realise their readers won't understand. You should also spot any missing words or unintentional repetitions at this stage.

Correcting the copy

This time, you are going to check the copy over carefully, five times, each time looking for something different.

1 **Spelling:** make sure each word is spelt correctly. Use a dictionary or a spellchecker to help you. (Beware spellcheckers though...)

2 **Punctuation:** check that the writer has put commas, fullstops and all other punctuation marks in the right places.

3 **Capitalisation:** make sure each sentence begins with a capital letter and that proper names also have capitals, and that no word has a capital letter when it shouldn't.

> ### Fun With Words 5
>
> Spellbound
>
> I have a spelling chequer
> It came with my PC
> It plainly marks four my revue
> Miss takes I cannot sea.
> I've run this poem threw it
> I'm shore your pleased too no;
> Its letter perfect in it's weigh
> My chequer tolled me sew.
>
> Nor Man Vandal

4 **Consistency:** make sure the writer hasn't changed tense or point of view without meaning to, and that characters' names and other proper nouns are spelt the same way each time.

5 **Paragraphing:** check that the writer has remembered to paragraph their work!

As you can see, a copyeditor needs a good eye for detail, good powers of concentration and the ability to spell and punctuate.

Finally, when your work is as well written and as correctly presented as possible, you can pat yourself on the back for having produced a masterpiece, at least in the old sense of the word!

Typography, Printing and Layout

Typography is the art of using typed letters effectively. It involves creative decisions by typographers and printers about the styles of letters, the size of letters and how to place them on the page in relation to each other, and in relation to the white space on the rest of the page. A masterly typographer will design a page so that it is easy to read and you will not notice their skilled input. If you find the 'look' of a piece of writing off-putting, then it may well be because it is poorly designed, perhaps with a difficult-to-read **font**, too small a type size and too little white space.

Producing printed text has been possible for only a few hundred years and many master craftsmen have been involved in this. Have

you ever thought about the people who *designed* the shapes of the letters you read?

The first commercial designer of typefaces was a Frenchman called Claude Garamond (1499–1561). His designs are still in use today, along with those from the 18th century by an Englishman, John Baskerville, and those of an Italian, Gambiasta Bodoni, who spent three years designing the letter 'A' of his Ultra typeface!

You can still find these surnames today – Garamond, Baskerville and Bodoni – in the list of fonts available on your computer. You can also find Century Bold, which was designed in 1890 by L B Benton, and Times New Roman which dates from 1931 and was designed by Stanley Morrison.

20th century technology transformed printing. It used to be a laborious task using individual letters made of lead which were then painstakingly assembled into words and lines of copy. Now, in the 21st century, if we type our work into a computer, we can all change our design instantly and create printed material with a single keystroke. Can you imagine what these ancient masters of typography would have thought of a computer?

Next time you are typing up your work, you might like to think about all the choices you have, literally, at your fingertips.

In addition to choosing your font, you can choose different *sizes* of letters. Type size is measured in points, a 300-year-old system. There are 72 points to an inch. Most copy in books is 11pt or 12pt for easy reading. Newspapers use a much bigger point size for headlines and a smaller point size, 10pt, for the stories so that they can get more words on the page. The main typeface in this book is Stone Serif and the typesize is 11pt.

You also have many more choices about the size of margins, the distance between each line of text and the addition of touches of bold or italic text for emphasis. Italics are called this because an *Italian* master craftsman called Aldo Manuzio first introduced this sloping type in 1501. (And we didn't even celebrate 500 years of italics in 2001!)

This is only the briefest of introductions to what is an ancient craft, which itself developed from religious manuscripts ('manu-script' means 'hand-written'). These were written very slowly by monks, and exquisitely decorated and illuminated with gold leaf. You may have heard of one, the Book of Kells, which dates from around the

late 6th century, or another, the Lindisfarne Gospels, from around a century later…

…and there we must leave this introduction to the craft of the writer. As your toolbox is only metaphorical, it should not be too heavy to carry forwards with you into the next part of this book!

Writer's Craft Toolkit Summary 8

You should now be familiar with the meaning and use of these editorial and printing tools:

- ✓ draft
- ✓ redraft
- ✓ copy
- ✓ copyediting
- ✓ typography
- ✓ font
- ✓ type size, points
- ✓ white space.

PART TWO

Writer's Craft Assessment Tasks

Introduction

The Writer's Craft tasks are used to assess your skills as apprentice imaginative writers.

Your task is to continue a piece of imaginative writing begun by another writer. You need to use and develop their characters, setting and events. You should also be trying to adopt the style, tone and atmosphere of the writer, while using spelling and punctuation as correctly as you can. (You can always use the passage itself as a good example of paragraphing, spelling and correct punctuation.)

You might think it should be easy to continue someone else's writing, but in order to do this you need three separate skills:

1 First, you need to be able to analyse the style and content of the writing.

2 Second, you have to absorb that 'feel' into your own mind: to adopt the mask or persona of that writer.

3 Third, you have to copy their style, making up events and perhaps characters to take the story forwards. You are not being asked to finish the story, only to continue for a few paragraphs.

The ability to put yourself in the head and pen of another writer is a useful skill to master: it will help you to find your own voice. In the same way, students of sport, art, fashion, music, or any other skill, will analyse and copy their heroes as part of their learning process.

It is important to realise that copying the style and content of another writer *in order to learn* is not **plagiarism**. Plagiarism (see page 41) is deliberate theft where you pretend you have written words that were written by someone else.

So, how do you continue someone else's writing? It's quite a challenging task that we will master in this part of the book.

We begin with a worked-through example of how to approach the Writer's Craft task. This includes a series of questions to help you analyse texts and to make you conscious of the techniques each writer is using. This is followed by ten examples for you to practise on.

After you've worked through the first five examples, you should find that you are able to mimic the style of different writers much more easily without having to rely on the analytical questions so heavily.

The first time you do this task will be the most difficult – it will become easier each time you practise. Honest!

Writer's Craft: Worked Example
The Ungrateful Queen

Joanne Deans

It was Monday and, like every other day, the queen was sitting on her golden throne, giving out orders. She sent Martha for her tea and scone.

'George, I want the newspaper! Oh, John, get my slippers, my feet are freezing!'

When she got that, she went on to send Martha, her head servant, to find a painter to do her portrait and George to find a tailor for a new coat. She was always moaning about how cold it was and how it was always raining. The fire was too low, the toast was too cold, the tea was too strong and the newspaper was even smudged. She was never happy.

As the days of winter rolled on, the queen got grumpier and grumpier. She sacked the gardener for the trees being bare. She now constantly moaned to George about the draught in the corridor, 'George, can you not stop that draught that constantly blows through the corridor? I get cold every time I go out there.'

However one day she had enough.

She called Martha over, 'I want to go away, to somewhere warm where there is always sun. I hate it here, anywhere must be better.'

Here's what you would be asked to do if this were a Writer's Craft Assessment Task:

Now continue the story. Try to match your choice of words and phrases and the way you put them together with that of the original author. Remember, you are not being asked to finish the story, or to bring it to any conclusion. This is a short piece of writing.

(From *National Assessments 5–14*, English Language, Writer's Craft)

Here is a way to approach the task using the following analytical questions.

First, read the passage again carefully. In the following worked example, the answers are supplied for you, but when you do this on your own, you will need to keep returning to the passage in order to answer the questions.

Analytical Questions with Answer Notes
The Ungrateful Queen

If you are unfamiliar with any of the terms here, you will find them explained in the first part of this book: The Writer's Toolkit.

1 What is the subject of this passage – that is, what is it about? Does the title give you a clue?

   Answer: a bad-tempered and ungrateful queen who is always complaining.

2 What is the writer's purpose? To entertain you? To inform you? To make you feel a particular emotion? To persuade you of something? To make you think?

   Answer: to entertain, and perhaps criticise someone who is ungrateful.

3 Who do you feel is the audience for this story – that is, who is it written for?

   Answer: perhaps children of about 8 or 9 upwards. Adults could enjoy it too.

4 What genre does it belong to? Fiction? What kind of fiction? Non-fiction? Poetry? What features of the writing identify the genre?

   Answer: fiction – fable or moral tale, because there seems to be a lesson for us here. It also feels a bit like a fairytale, with a queen and a 'golden throne', but there doesn't seem to be any magic or fairies.

5 What register is the writer using? Formal or informal? Standard English or dialect?

   Answer: formal, standard English.

6 How would you describe the kind of vocabulary the writer uses? Are the words long or short, simple or complex, poetic or technical or what?

   Answer: quite simple.

7 Are there many adjectives or adverbs?

Answer: no, a few, but not a lot.

8 How does the writer construct their sentences and paragraphs? Are they long or short, simple or complex, statements or questions or a mixture?

Answer: some long, some short sentences, one very short paragraph as a turning point. Mostly statements or orders from the queen.

9 What tense has the writer used? Past or present?

Answer: past tense.

10 Do you notice any distinctive use of punctuation, other than the usual commas, speech marks and fullstops?

Answer: no, not really, maybe the semi-colon in the third paragraph.

11 Do you see any patterns or repetitions in the writing? What effect do they have?

Answer: yes. Too... too... too... and 'always' twice, 'constantly' twice, 'grumpier' twice. For humour, for emphasis and to make sound patterns.

12 Has the writer used first, second or third person narration?

Answer: third person narration.

13 What is the pace of the writing? How quickly or slowly is it moving along?

Answer: quite quickly. 'As the days of winter rolled on...'.

14 Is the writer using direct speech?

Answer: yes, but only the queen actually speaks so far.

15 What literary devices or figures of speech is the writer using? Simile or metaphor? Personification?

*Answer: one metaphor, the winter days 'rolled on' as if they actually **were** big wheels.*

16 Is the writer deliberately using sound effects? Onomatopoeia, alliteration, or long or short vowels for effect?

Answer: long vowels, like moaning, when the queen is complaining about the draught.

17 Where is the story happening? Can you add any details about the place?

Answer: there is a cold draughty palace and a garden, although the story looks like it might be shifting to somewhere warmer.

18 What kind of characters has the writer created? Are they major or minor characters? What kinds of names do they have? Are the characters unusual in any way? Do they have a problem?

Answer: major characters – queen, Martha, George. Minor characters – gardener. Names – ordinary fairly modern names. The queen is unusual because she is so bad-tempered and she has created a problem (wanting to go somewhere warm and sunny) that Martha, and perhaps George, are expected to solve.

19 What does the plot seem to be – that is, what's happening? What could happen next?

Answer: we have a cold and bad-tempered queen who doesn't seem to appreciate anything she has. Maybe she could change her attitude and learn to be grateful? Maybe she will be punished for being ungrateful? Maybe she will realise that other things are more important? Maybe she'll move somewhere warmer?

20 Is there any humour, black or otherwise?

Answer: sacking the gardener because the leaves have fallen off the trees!

21 And finally, what would you say the theme is?

Answer: discontentment, annoyance, selfishness, ill-humour.

Writer's Craft Task

The Ungrateful Queen

Now continue the story. Try to match your choice of words and phrases and the way you put them together with that of the original author. Remember, you are not being asked to finish the story, or to bring it to any conclusion. This is a short piece of writing.

By answering as many of the analytical questions as we can, we become much more conscious of the content and style of this piece of writing that we now have to continue.

There are many ways to continue this story using Joanne's characters, plot and her style. Each of us would do it differently but

here is Joanne's original text plus one possible continuation that tries to develop much of what she has already established.

See if you can spot the join – it should be invisible!

The Ungrateful Queen

It was Monday, and like every other day, the queen was sitting on her golden throne, giving out orders. She sent Martha for her tea and scone.

'George, I want the newspaper! Oh, John, get my slippers, my feet are freezing!'

When she got that, she went on to send Martha, her head servant, to find a painter to do her portrait and George to find a tailor for a new coat. She was always moaning about how cold it was and how it was always raining. The fire was too low, the toast was too cold, the tea was too strong and the newspaper was even smudged. She was never happy.

As the days of winter rolled on, the queen got grumpier and grumpier. She sacked the gardener for the trees being bare. She now constantly moaned to George about the draught in the corridor, 'George, can you not stop that draught that constantly blows through the corridor? I get cold every time I go out there.'

However one day she had enough.

She called Martha over, 'I want to go away, to somewhere warm where there is always sun. I hate it here, anywhere must be better.'

Martha had never seen the queen so bad-tempered and she felt a little afraid.

She hurried down to the village to ask the advice of Samuel, an old sailor who had travelled the world.

'I'd recommend a journey to the South Pole,' he said, with a mischievous twinkle in his blue eyes. 'That would teach her majesty what cold really is! And she could see how well the albatrosses and the emperor penguins live down that way!'

'Oh no!' said Martha, shivering at the thought. 'That would be too awful! I don't much like the cold either, although it would be nice to see albatrosses and penguins.'

➤

59

'Alright, I have the perfect solution. Listen while I tell you what to do...'

When Martha came back, quite a long time later, the queen was very angry.

'Where have you been all this time? Get me some fresh tea immediately to warm me up! Make sure it's weak! And before you go, have you found me somewhere warm where the sun shines all day?'

Martha nodded and was about to speak when the queen interrupted her.

'Pack my trunks immediately! We leave tonight.'

You can see how this continuation includes Martha, introduces a new character (the old sailor), extends the sense of place to include a village and the South Pole, and moves the plot forwards by appearing to come up with a solution, which probably won't be the one the queen wants! The queen also reappears, still bad-tempered. Her demand for weak tea, her complaint about the cold, and the way she is still ordering Martha about, all link back to Joanne's writing. The story is still far from finished.

If you *really* want to check how well you've picked up on the craft of the writer, answer the same analytical questions for your continuation! Your answers should be very similar to those you noted for the actual passage.

You might also find that, having put so much work into becoming able to continue the story, you don't want to stop! This is a good sign, and evidence that your creative powers are working. Your own stories will become better and easier to write as a result.

Writer's Craft Assessment Tasks

Here is the first of ten Writer's Craft Assessment Tasks for you to try. Use the analytical questions that follow it to help you.

Some of the answers will be easy and obvious to you and others will make you think. Remember, you can always look back to the first part of this book to refresh your memory if there are any technical terms you don't understand.

Practice Text 1
Red Bird

Valerie Thornton

Once upon a time, many long years ago, in a far-distant, green land, there lived a bird with feathers as bright as the reddest of poppies.

Red Bird was happy there and spent his days hopping around in the sunshine looking for brown seeds or yellow fruits that he could feast on.

'Chip-chip-chip, tralee!' he would sing. 'Another fine day for me!'

He had many friends, including Blue Bird, White Mouse, Golden Frog and Silver Fish. He would tell them where to find the best food and where the sunniest places to snooze were.

'Chip-chip-chip, tralee!' he would sing. 'Come and follow me!'

But one day Red Bird had a problem.

The roof of his little old house had fallen in. He hopped sadly from one red foot to the other, looking at the jumble of brown twigs and green moss and moulted feathers as bright as the reddest of poppies that had once been his home.

'Chip-chip-chip, traloo!' he sang mournfully. 'What am I going to do?'

Then he decided to go and ask for help.

Before you begin your Writer's Craft task of continuing this story, here are the analytical questions (without any answers this time) to help you.

Read the passage again before you begin to answer them and refer back to the passage often as you work through them. Remember to make brief notes only. You don't have to answer every single question, but the more answers you can come up with, the more helpful you will find it.

Analytical Questions

1 What is the subject of this passage – that is, what is it about? Does the title give you a clue?

2 What is the writer's purpose? To entertain you? To inform you? To make you feel a particular emotion? To persuade you of something? To make you think?

3 Who do you feel is the audience for this story – that is, who is it written for?

4 What genre does it belong to? Fiction? What kind of fiction? Non-fiction? Poetry? What features of the writing identify the genre?

5 What register is the writer using? Formal or informal? Standard English or dialect?

6 How would you describe the kind of vocabulary the writer uses? Are the words long or short, simple or complex, poetic or technical or what?

7 Are there many adjectives or adverbs?

8 How does the writer construct their sentences and paragraphs? Are they long or short, simple or complex, statements or questions or a mixture?

9 What tense has the writer used? Past or present?

10 Do you notice any distinctive use of punctuation, other than the usual commas, speech marks and full stops?

11 Do you see any patterns or repetitions in the writing? What effect do they have?

12 Has the writer used first, second or third person narration?

13 What is the pace of the writing? How quickly or slowly is it moving along?

14 Is the writer using direct speech?

15 What literary devices or figures of speech is the writer using? Simile or metaphor? Personification?

16 Is the writer deliberately using sound effects? Onomatopoeia, alliteration, or long or short vowels for effect?

17 Where is the story happening? Can you add any details about the place?

18 What kind of characters has the writer created? Are they major or minor characters? What kinds of names do they have? Are the characters unusual in any way? Do they have a problem?

19 What does the plot seem to be – that is, what's happening? What could happen next?

20 Is there any humour, black or otherwise?

21 And finally, what would you say the theme is?

You should be ready to do your Writer's Craft task for 'Red Bird', which is:

Now continue the story. Try to match your choice of words and phrases and the way you put them together with that of the original author. Remember, you are not being asked to finish the story, or to bring it to any conclusion. This is a short piece of writing.

Practice Text 2
Getting Sent For
Donald Hutton

In primary school, there was nothing better than a good fight. My usual sparring partner was Stephen but he was still in the dining hall trying to force down his chocolate custard. I always thought that pudding should be a treat at the end of the meal, something to be enjoyed. In Port Charlotte School, a pudding often doubled as a punishment.

'Your parents have paid good money for this food and you'll finish it... all!' Mrs Don would harp as she loomed over us till we finished it... all.

I was able to spoon most of my custard into my cousin Duncan's bowl when the old witch's back was turned. He actually likes the stuff! Stephen on the other hand was not so lucky. So while the tears rolled down his cheeks as he forced down his poison, I was in the playground looking for an adversary.

I found just the person, Robbie Jackson; he was always into a good scuffle and usually didn't take too much goading.

Before you begin your Writer's Craft task of continuing this story, read Donald's writing again.

Then, look back at the Analytical Questions (page 62) to help you. Keep referring back to Donald's writing as you work through them. Remember to make brief notes only and try to answer every question.

Now continue the story. Try to match your choice of words and phrases and the way you put them together with that of the original author. Remember, you are not being asked to finish the story, or to bring it to any conclusion. This is a short piece of writing.

Practice Text 3
Thowar Boway
Stuart McLardie

I opened the small detailed wooden container, which was shaped as a small person. It was quite like an Indian with a yellow mask. Nothing happened. I had unscrewed the top fully but still nothing happened.

All of a sudden a large dark cloud of smoke drifted out and formed a large silver figure about eight feet tall. It almost looked like metal.

'Who are you?' said the large silver creature. 'You have set me free from my eternal sleep. BIG MISTAKE, but since it was you who set me free, I shall spare you and your family.'

The silver creature headed for the door.

'Stop!' I said, 'What are you?'

He said, 'I am Thowar Boway and king from my home plain of Lyrinea.'

What I saw next was horrifying. Thowar stepped out onto the street and stood in front of an old lady.

'Aaaarrgh!' I heard the old woman cry as she was picked up, ripped in two and eaten.

I couldn't let this monster run wild and I called my friend Colin to help. We must defeat it.

Before you begin your Writer's Craft task of continuing this story, read Stuart's writing again.

Then, look back at the Analytical Questions (page 62) to help you. Keep referring back to Stuart's writing as you work through them. Remember to make brief notes only and try to answer every question.

Now continue the story. Try to match your choice of words and phrases and the way you put them together with that of the original author. Remember, you are not being asked to finish the story, or to bring it to any conclusion. This is a short piece of writing.

Practice Text 4
Determination

Richard McQuarrie

He was alone, the only person left in the changing room. He was reflecting on what his parents had said. 'It doesn't matter if you don't win, son. It only matters that you try your best.' He knew that was just what they said. They were really desperate for him to win. Who wanted a son who was head of the science club instead of captain of the football team? His parents had been overjoyed when their son, their embarrassment of a son, had shown a flair for running. He took his glasses off and put them in his locker with the rest of his stuff. He was ready, or at least he hoped he was.

He walked out the tunnel and onto the playing field. He felt sick, he was so nervous. He had to win. This was his chance to prove himself, to show that he wasn't just a geek. He looked at all the people ready to compete in the sports day events. They were the strong-legged long jumpers, the agile high jumpers, the quick female runners and their admirers, the tough rugby players and the skilful footballers. The clouds were dark as if to foretell events to come.

The crowd had begun to gather. Somewhere among them were his parents. His father had taken time off work to watch him. He knew how much his dad wanted him to win. He had been a football player and would tell anyone who would listen about his sporting days. Now he wrote sports articles for a big newspaper. He didn't really know how to connect with his dad; he felt like such a disappointment.

Before you begin your Writer's Craft task of continuing this story, read Richard's writing again.

Then, look back at the Analytical Questions (page 62) to help you. Keep referring back to Richard's writing as you work through them. Remember to make brief notes only and try to answer every question.

Now continue the story. Try to match your choice of words and phrases and the way you put them together with that of the original author. Remember, you are not being asked to finish the story, or to bring it to any conclusion. This is a short piece of writing.

Practice Text 5
Answer Me
Sarah Reynolds

Can you spare me a dream, Mister? A wee morsel like a ray of hope in a paper bag, or a smile perhaps. Anything like that would do. There's the moon above these shops you know, stars laughing, foxes in the park, a winter pansy fighting back in the gutter by the bin there. Just like me.

You've no time for looking though, have you?

You've walked through the Botanics feeling smart about yourself. All Burberry swish and the right carrier bags on display. It's not cold enough to fasten your coat buttons so you can let your GAP sweater hang out and the west end world won't brand you a total stuffed shirt. You're looking in that window and the last thing on your mind's the price. Unless it is too cheap of course. Cause and effect. Price is just about the only thing you don't consider – there's nothing much not calculated about you. You don't angle an eyebrow without making sure it's on your good side.

You've never been hungry in your life, have you?

Before you begin your Writer's Craft task of continuing this story, read Sarah's writing again.

Then, look back at the Analytical Questions (page 62) to help you. Keep referring back to Sarah's writing as you work through them. Remember to make brief notes only and try to answer every question.

Now continue the story. Try to match your choice of words and phrases and the way you put them together with that of the original author. Remember, you are not being asked to finish the story, or to bring it to any conclusion. This is a short piece of writing.

You have now had the opportunity to practise the Writer's Craft task on five separate and very different pieces of writing.

Here are five more pieces. See if you can do them without the help of the Analytical Questions. You should still read the passage several times and make notes for yourself. If you're lucky, you will find that you have absorbed much of the technique for doing this task. If not, then you can still look back to the Analytical Questions on page 62 to help you.

Practice Text 6
The Meteor Shower
Valerie Thornton

As Commander K'lan B'losk raced to the upper deck of Galaxy Surfer II, all he could see around him through the 50cm thick astro-glass was meteors. Large and small, near and far, hurtling towards his spaceship, trailing angry plumes of burning space dust.

It was a bad time for a meteor shower. Vice-Commander M'ata T'orsk was down in the force suite trying her best to fix the sudden leak in Galaxy Surfer II's meteor-deflection zone. The other two crew members were deep in an astro-sleep.

There was always the emergency life-ship but Commander K'lan B'losk didn't want to admit defeat just yet. Galaxy Surfer I had been lost to a similar meteor shower and for Commander K'lan B'losk to lose a second ship would be unthinkable.

Perhaps the other two crew members could help? Or maybe he should recall Vice-Commander M'ata T'orsk? He looked again at the shower of meteors exploding towards him.

He didn't like what he saw.

He flicked open his emergency astro-phone and spoke urgently into it.

Now continue the story. Try to match your choice of words and phrases and the way you put them together with that of the original author. Remember, you are not being asked to finish the story, or to bring it to any conclusion. This is a short piece of writing.

Practice Text 7
The Challenge

Rebecca Low

– Who's the new kid?

The words filled the air.

– Who's the new kid?

The murmurs buzzed, and word of the new kid spread around the playground like wildfire.

– Who is the new kid?

No one knew who he was or where he came from.

Except Paddy. He knew.

The words stung him like hot irons, burning the words 'new kid' onto his forehead. Paddy lowered his head as he walked across the playground, hating the eyes that were staring at him, boring holes into the back of his head, wishing they would all go away.

It wasn't his fault that he was the new kid. It wasn't his fault that his father was in the army. He couldn't help it that he moved school every few months.

Paddy sighed and scuffed the ground with the toe of his trainer. It was going to be a long day.

He sat at the very back of the class and didn't answer any of the teacher's questions. He kept his head down and his mouth shut. After school (and a lecture from his mother about the state of his trainers), Paddy went down to the sea and sat on the beach. He hugged his knees to his chin and closed his eyes. He felt so alone, so isolated on that lonely beach. The warm, evening breeze ruffled his hair.

He imagined a beach full of children, screaming and yelling with delight. He heard their cries. They sounded so real. Paddy opened his eyes.

Over on the rocks he saw ten or so children about his age, shouting and yelling and laughing as they scrambled over the rocks and boulders. Paddy rubbed his eyes, checking that he wasn't still dreaming. No, they were definitely real.

He stood up and smiled to himself. At last, he thought, someone to play with. He bounded over the pebbly beach and stopped when he reached the rocks.

Now continue the story. Try to match your choice of words and phrases and the way you put them together with that of the original author. Remember, you are not being asked to finish the story, or to bring it to any conclusion. This is a short piece of writing.

Practice Text 8
A Midwinter Night's Dream
Margaret Walker

It always began with the same beginning, but the ending was always different.

I sit at my desk with a blank page before me. I can't write. I have no inspiration. I can gradually feel myself being overtaken by sleep. Yes, that's what I want: good, deep sleep – safe sleep.

Then the noise comes. The eerie, otherworldly howling from the surrounding moors. It is one of those sounds which is impossible to describe in words; not the howling of a ravenous wolf, and definitely not the shrieks of a child or baby or distressed woman. This howling is made by... something else, something deeper, more ancient.

I lift my head and open my window. There, out on the dark, silent moors stands a female figure, cloaked and hooded. The hood hides her face in the shadow, but her lengthy locks sway gently in the breeze. I can't see the colour of her hair, or her facial features – but a tear is caught by the Moon's delicate, pale fingers, illuminating this single tear and filling it with an unseen, crepuscular* magic. 'Come inside! You look frozen to death!' I cry.

The figure shakes her head in silence, but doesn't leave.

* 'crepuscular' is a word of Latin origin meaning 'twilight'

Now continue the story. Try to match your choice of words and phrases and the way you put them together with that of the original author. Remember, you are not being asked to finish the story, or to bring it to any conclusion. This is a short piece of writing.

Practice Text 9
The Magpie's Secret
Kathleen Daly

It is some years now since I heard my grandfather recite the old superstition:

One for sorrow
Two for joy
Three for a wedding
Four for a boy
Five for silver
Six for gold
And seven for a secret
That never was told.

It had a deep effect on my life. It was after I had been stoned by some schoolboys as they chanted, 'Go home, and take your sorrow with you!' that he explained it to me.

'Better to travel with a group of friends,' he said. 'You are in less danger from humans.'

I did not heed his advice, for I am a loner by choice. Not that I don't enjoy the *crack*, but there is a certain satisfaction in travelling alone that being in company misses out on. For instance, I can get closer to humans when I'm alone, especially when they don't know I'm there. I have heard many dialects and they would be surprised if they knew how easily I *pick up the patter*, as they say.

Also, we have one thing in common: we like bright baubles. They like to display theirs on their person (jewellery they call it), arousing envy in their friends. I on the other hand, preferred to grace my own little special place with them, enjoying their beauty in secret.

My method of acquiring those dazzling delights is very simple. In the early morning I sally forth, leisurely alighting on each promising-looking windowsill and you would be surprised how many of the windows are open. To let in fresh air, I presume. Well, when I'm around it lets me in also, and as my tribe have been light-clawed for

years, I've inherited my deftness for extracting the loveliest treasures for myself.

I freely confess that in the beginning, part of my fun was staying within earshot or returning later to hear the hullabaloo the wife made on discovering her loss. One would think she had lost an arm or leg. Every time I look upon the baubles I relive this, and dance about in delight.

There was, however, one occasion when I was not proud of my feat. An easy pickup it turned out to be. A drawer lying open in an empty bedroom and a single gold ring lying carelessly within, as if it was waiting for me. My movements were quick and silent and this time I didn't linger but hurried home.

Now continue the story. Try to match your choice of words and phrases and the way you put them together with that of the original author. Remember, you are not being asked to finish the story, or to bring it to any conclusion. This is a short piece of writing.

Practice Text 10

(You will notice that this last example is slightly different from the others but, nonetheless, by now you should have mastered the technique for continuing it.)

Looking after Your Bicycle

At least once a year, you should give your bicycle a thorough check to make sure it is in good working order. (Remember: your life could depend on it!)

There are many important parts to a bicycle – the tyres, the wheels, the chain, the gears, the saddle, the frame, but perhaps the most important is your braking system.

First, have a good look at the brakes. Check that the brake blocks are not worn and needing replaced. Also check that the cables and levers are clean and are moving smoothly. Adjust the blocks so that they are only a few millimetres clear of the wheel rims. Spin each wheel to check that it is running freely. (Remember: the less distance the blocks have to travel, the faster you'll stop!)

Then test the brakes carefully to make sure your bike stops promptly, even when you are going fast. (Remember: always use the back brake first or else you will go over the handlebars!)

When you are sure that your brakes can save your life, move on to check the next part of your bicycle.

Now continue this piece of writing. Try to match your choice of words and phrases and the way you put them together with that of the original author. Remember, you are not being asked to finish it, or to bring it to any conclusion. This is a short piece of writing.

PART THREE

Masterpieces

Introduction

You will remember from Part One of this book (page 20) that the meaning of the word *masterpiece* has changed over the hundreds of years that it's been in use.

Long ago, a masterpiece was like the present-day equivalent of a trial for a football team or an audition for a singing, dancing or acting part.

Now, we understand it to mean a superb piece of work from someone who is already a master at what they are doing.

The short stories, poems and autobiography in the final part of this book are good enough to deserve the modern meaning of *masterpiece*.

After each piece of writing, you will find questions to help you appreciate it. (If you want to increase your technical appreciation of each masterpiece, you can use the Analytical Questions from Part Two to guide you too).

You will then be encouraged to produce your own masterpiece. You might feel less daunted if you think of the original meaning of the word. Perhaps, though, your work might fit into both old and new categories! You might also like to look back to the guiding questions in the Drafting and Redrafting section in Part One (page 47) to help you.

You will also find photographs between each masterpiece. These images deliberately have no explanations so that you can react creatively to them in whatever way you want. Look carefully at whichever image interests you and see what questions arise in your mind. They might lead you to an autobiographical memory, or a short story, or a poem. If you want to kick-start a creative response, you can ask yourself the following questions: Who? What? Where? Why? When? How? And then answer them…!

The Snake's Wishes

Rachael Cassidy's Masterpiece

In a small town long ago, there lived a writer. He was kind and friendly but did not have much success or money and few publishers wanted his books. He lived in a small, neat house close to the zoo, which was kept by his brother. The zoo was his favourite place to be and he visited it frequently when he had the time. Around the time of this story, however, he had not been going to the zoo as often as usual because his mother was ill and he had been visiting her instead.

One bright morning he had just left his mother's house and was about to go home, when he decided to have a walk around the zoo instead. After he paid the tiny admission fee to the man at the gate, he headed for the zoo's reptile enclosure. Immediately, he realised there was a new snake, which was odd as the zoo rarely got new animals. It was bright red with black diamonds along its back and big yellow eyes. It slithered right up to the glass and opened its mouth to hiss at the writer, baring its glistening fangs. But no hiss came out – instead the snake spoke in a deep resonating voice.

'Greetings,' the snake said smoothly. 'As you can see I am no ordinary snake – I possess great magical power. I have decided, in order to prove my greatness to you, that I will grant you three wishes.'

'W-well...' stammered the man, who was unsure of what to say. 'Perhaps you could cure my mother, because she is very ill and I'm worried about her.'

'Perhaps!' the snake raged. 'My power is greater than that. You should ask for something bigger and more important, like a castle or thousands of pounds. Make a second wish.'

The man thought for a moment.

'Every week on my way to the zoo, I pass lots of poor people sitting in the street. They have no homes or money and they all look hungry. Use your magic to help them.'

The snake's eyes flashed angrily.

'What a stupid wish!' it sneered. 'What kind of fool would ask for something like that when he can have anything in the world? Ask to be a powerful emperor, or a famous sorcerer, or the richest man on earth. These are the things that really matter.'

The man shook his head.

'I can't ask for those things. But I do have one more wish you could grant. Two of my friends have had a fight. Neither will speak to the other and both say it's the other's fault. Use your magic and make them friends again.'

This time the snake said nothing. It glared at the man for the next few seconds until an orange flame leapt up and engulfed it. In a cloud of smoke, the snake disappeared and the flame died down.

The bemused writer blinked a couple of times, then turned and went home. Nothing had changed: his mother was still sick, the peasants were still poor and his friends still hated each other.

A few days later, however, he wrote down the story of his strange encounter and sent it to a publisher. It became hugely popular and made him a lot of money. Some of this money he spent on hiring the best doctor in the country for his mother, who soon recovered. Some of it went on building homes for the poor people he used to walk past. And his two friends both read the story and consequently made up and remained friends all their lives.

The writer, in short, lived a happy and prosperous existence for the rest of his days.

Rachael's inspiration

Most of the writing in this book has been written by adults. However, Rachael wrote this story when she was only 13. Rachael's inspiration came from after-school creative writing workshops in which she studied both 'Jacob's Chicken' (page 92) and a short story called 'The Golden Fish' which was written by a Russian writer called Alexander Pushkin almost 200 years ago. In the latter story, a golden fish grants the increasingly greedy wishes of a cruel and selfish old woman until she makes too big a wish (to control the golden fish herself) and the golden fish reverses everything and returns her to her original poverty.

While some pupils produced a different piece of writing each week, Rachael spent several weeks working away on this one story. She acknowledged the fable/moral tale and fairy tale genre and, at the same time, moved it forwards into a fresh and masterly interpretation with a very modern feel.

Questions

 ## Appreciating this masterpiece

Why is the hero's occupation witty and appropriate here? What are more normal occupations for heroes and heroines of fairy stories?

Rachael sets up three elements of the storyline in the first paragraph. What are they?

In the second paragraph, there is a turning point when the writer decides to do something different: instead of going home, he goes to the zoo. He is then surprised, twice. By what?

What does the snake say in his first speech that places this story firmly in the fairy tale genre? What hint do we get about the character of the snake? Why is he offering the writer three wishes?

What is unusual about the writer's wishes? What do people normally wish for in fairy tales? Think of three words to describe the writer's character.

What is unusual about the snake's reaction to each wish? What does the snake think *is* worth having? Think of three words to describe the snake's character.

Rachael has put two masterly turning points into the plot of the story in the last two paragraphs. What are they?

What purpose does the snake serve in the plot of this story?

Some stories are written purely because the writer wants to entertain us. Others, like 'Jacob's Chicken', are written because the writer also wants their story to make a bigger point. In these stories, the characters also symbolise something else, for example, the adults in 'Jacob's Chicken' symbolise pompous and ignorant authority.

What bigger point is Rachael making here about values? What does the snake symbolise here? What does a snake symbolise in our wider culture?

How modern (or timeless) is the desire for wealth and power? Are there characters with the same attitudes and values as Rachael's snake still around today? What *do* people wish for these days? What do *you* wish for?

(Is there not something very satisfying in Rachael writing a story about a writer who would like to be published, and Rachael herself now finding that same wish coming true for herself here?)

Three masterly techniques used by Rachael

1 Choosing an unusual hero for a fairytale.
2 Adding a masterly twist to the usual three-wishes story.
3 Devising a very effective ending.

Your masterpiece

Here's your big chance to make wishes come true, at least on the page!

Think of a character who is unhappy because something is missing or wrong in their life or in the world around them. Make lots of notes and don't settle for your first ideas, either of the character or of what is wrong. Your character can be human, or some other creature... anything at all (but not a snake!).

Then think of a magic creature or object that can talk and can grant up to three wishes. Rachael created a good hero and a bad snake. Think about whether you want your two main characters to be both good, both bad, or one of each. Explore how each possibility could affect your plot. Maybe one of your characters could change from bad to good, or vice versa, by the end?

Decide what your ending is before you start to write: happy ever after, or not? Then you will know where your plot is going.

Before she started, Rachael worked out that her writer's wishes would come true at the end, but she managed to make it seem as if they wouldn't.

If you want to be really ambitious, then decide on a message you want your story to give to your readers. You can give your tale a **moral**, which is like a lesson that the story illustrates. For example, the moral in Rachael's story might be, 'if you try to help others, you too will be rewarded' or 'there are a greater things in life than money or power'.

You might find inspiration by creating a bad character who is boastful, angry, jealous, greedy or lazy. Or a good character who might be optimistic, generous, fair, brave or kind.

Write your story in the style of a fairytale. Your opening words will be easy, as the place and time are always far away. Why do you think fairy tales are distanced from here and now?

Look back at Rachael's sentences. They are short and fairly simple, another feature of the fairy tale genre. Why do you think this is? Who are fairytales mainly written for it?

Take your time and think your ideas through first, making as many notes as you want. Enjoy your power as a writer to wave your magic wand and make whatever you want happen in your story!

My Last Day at School

Michael Chromy's Masterpiece

The world hadn't always been like this. Back through Cenozoic, Mesozoic, Palaeozoic to Precambrian. It was different then. Volcanoes ruptured barren landscapes and the world stank of sulphur. Sea worms threaded their way through crinoids and sponges on the ocean floor. Ammonites spiralled around giant murky sea scorpions. Land masses plated up on each other while cockroaches and millipedes began to colonise the planet. Fire and ice. Dinosaurs eventually roaming around right where I was sitting. It must have been brilliant. I wish I'd been alive then.

My mum sat in the chair where she always sat. She was still in her sickly blue water-stained dressing gown. She was ill. She had to rest a lot. She'd probably been sitting there all day watching the telly. She went on watching the telly and didn't even answer when I spoke. Her face just made expressions which said things like 'that's interesting' or 'really?' or 'later'. She was dead quiet these days. She hardly ever said anything. She might as well have just slept twenty-four hours a day. I went into the kitchen to look for something to eat and to draw pictures of dinosaurs. There was an eruption of dirty dishes in the sink. Grease had dripped and congealed on dinner plates. I made a crater with some dirty dreggy cups and fast flowing liquid lava trails ran down quickly to the soupy broth which lay at the bottom of the brown basin. The bin was overflowing and stinking so I gathered it all up and took it out and emptied it into the big bin at the back door. On the kitchen table a T. Rex fought a bloody battle with a Stegosaurus. There was only ever going to be one winner.

I took the pictures into school the next day. Our teacher, Theropod, said she'd put them on the wall. But she never did. She put them on her table and hissed that I could take a sweet. She always had sweets in a clear plastic jar on her table. Sometimes I used to just sit and stare at them. She used them as bait. They were brilliant colours and all mixed up and piled up on top of each other. I could see marshmallow twists and flying saucers and others wrapped up in shiny paper. You got one if you deserved it. You always got what you deserved in this class. I kept my sweet in my pocket till we were outside in the drizzly rain and then I held it out to Amy. Her eyes went wide and we laughed. I wasn't sure why. Maybe we were laughing at different things.

After playtime we got out our reading books. Theropod stalked about the room. When it was Amy's turn to read I wished I could trace the words out into her head for her. She was slow and made mistakes and the teacher didn't give her enough time. I wished she would stop shouting at her. I wished the others in the pack would stop laughing.

There was an incident during lunch. After we were back in class the teacher told Beckie and Amy to stand beside her table. Beckie had got some fresh clothes from the store and was holding her own muddied garb in a plastic bag. When Theropod asked Beckie what happened she just started squealing again. Amy was vulnerable. No hiding place, no camouflage. I tried to think of a way to save her. Theropod went mad. Beckie was like Theropod's own child. It was like a chance she'd been waiting for. Theropod circled Amy, going on and on and on. Ripping her apart. Amy looked so small. She just stared at the floor. I had to do something. I lied. I told Theropod that Beckie had started it. I told her that Beckie had called her a name and then struck the first blow.

'What name?' she growled, as her eyes went to the ceiling then swooped down. You're a liar, her expression said. I stayed calm.

'A bad name, Miss. A really bad name,' I said. I didn't know whether I was going to say it. If I could say it. The Theropod rose up

in front of me. She was twenty feet tall, her tail flicking back and forth behind her.

'What name?' she roared, 'What name?' Her head began to slowly rotate around a stationary point right between her eyes. She waited for my reply. My heart was thudding. I could smell her breath.

I said the name. A long, long time ago at another school, in another place, someone else got called a name. Everybody had heard it. Even the master. The culprit was never seen or heard of again. I could think of nothing else. I said that Amy had been called the same name. She looked at me, her head cocked to one side. I thought for a minute she was going to burst out laughing. She sent Amy to the Lizard King and then she hissed that what I'd just said would get somebody into a lot of trouble. I knew by her proximity and the smell of her breath who it was going to be.

My mum asked what I had done at school. I lied. She turned her head to look over at me. Then she smiled and said she was really tired and could I not talk to her just now. She sounded funny. She had got dressed though and there was some new stuff in the fridge. I wished she'd get better. I thought she would have got better when my dad went away. But she didn't. In fact, she got worse.

I went out to play like I always did. I ran over the road and through the hole in the fence and into the park. Near the trees there was a place you could sit between the fence and the hedge and watch everybody. Nobody could see you. Two big ones came in for a drink. I watched them wander around and then head over to a group of younger ones who scattered as they approached. The two big ones sat on a bench and tossed the big brown bottle they'd been drinking from. Then they started pushing each other. Like dinosaurs. The one with the shaved head pushed the other one down and then they started fighting. They thrashed around and rolled down into a gully. The one who'd started it got up first and sank his teeth into the throat of the other one who was still lying on the ground. He never got up again. There was blood everywhere. The shaved head dragged the other one's lifeless body off into the bushes and ate it.

It was dark when I got home. The light was still on in the living room but there was no noise from the telly. I thought at first my mum must have gone to bed but then I heard voices. She was talking to somebody. I waited in the kitchen till the voice was gone. My mum came into the kitchen with an empty glass. I noticed she was in her dressing gown again. I asked her who that had been. She didn't answer.

She started asking me weird stuff and talking about things I didn't understand. I told her to stop but she wouldn't. I felt scared. She said everything would be all right. I said, 'What are you talking about?' She went to bed. She shouted down, 'Just stick around – okay? Everything'll be fine. Just be here.'

I wanted to go upstairs but I was too scared. I fell asleep watching the telly and woke up in the middle of the night. It was dead quiet. As I crept upstairs I thought I heard something. Like a cough. I stopped outside her door to listen. I must have imagined it. There was nothing.

The next day it was pouring. Even though I ran all the way to school I was still late. I didn't even go to the shop. Amy wasn't in. Neither was our teacher. It was the Lizard King. He told me it would be a while before I'd be seeing my pal again. Then another teacher I'd never seen before came in and he went away. The new teacher had scaly skin and claws which were curved like sickles. I could smell her. Like iron. Like blood. Amy's empty chair drew her attention. She came over for a closer look. I felt like she was trying to hypnotise me. Beckie smiled across from her clearing, all safe.

I was starving. I wished now I had just gone to the shop. My mum had still been sleeping when I left. I didn't try to wake her up. I didn't even go into her room. I didn't have time. When I left the house I pulled the door gently shut behind me. A woman who lived across the road waved at me as usual as I ran past.

The Sickle told us our normal teacher would be back tomorrow. She was still digesting Amy. It had stopped raining by playtime. I went round the back of the school on my own and waited. Nobody even noticed. I just stood there. The noise of everybody else in the

playground was drifting over the roof and seemed to be coming from the sky. I looked up and watched all the different shades of grey moving at different speeds. I kept on looking. I wondered who would ever trace out the answers for Amy now. I thought about my mum. A bell rang in the sky and I listened to the noise from the playground slowly deaden in silence. I started to shiver. I stayed where I was.

I got back home and unlocked the door. I knew right away. I went up the stairs and stood outside her room. I couldn't hear anything so I slowly pushed the door open. She was lying with her face to the wall. The curtains were still shut. I walked over and said her name but she didn't answer. I sat on the bed but she didn't move. I leant over and pushed her hair off her face. Her skin was cold. I climbed in beside her. I had to heat her up. Fire and ice. It made no difference what happened millions of years ago. It was still the same. The world had always been like this. Always would be. I put my arms around my mum and whispered, 'I'm here.'

Questions

Appreciating this masterpiece

This short story has an unusual start. The first paragraph (apart from the last three sentences) reads like a completely different genre of writing. What genre could this also be? Give three examples of words or phrases that belonged to this other genre.

How does the narration change in the third last sentence of this paragraph to return us to short story genre?

Why do you think the narrator wishes he'd been alive then, rather than now?

He has his head in two worlds, prehistoric and present. Quote three words in paragraph 2 that connect the mess in the kitchen sink with the volcanoes mentioned in paragraph 1.

Do you think 'Theropod' is his teacher's real name? Why did he call her this? What does his use of the word 'hissed' add to our perception of the teacher?

Find two more words in the paragraph beginning, 'After playtime we got out our reading books...' that dehumanise both the teacher and the pupils. What do they become?

The narrator feels very protective towards Amy to the extent of lying to save her. Why do you think this is?

Look at what happens to his perception of the teacher when she focuses her anger on him instead of on Amy. Normally, the teacher is referred to as Theropod. Can you explain what changes when Michael, the writer, adds the definite article before 'Theropod' in the paragraph beginning, 'A bad name, Miss...'? Can you identify with this transformation when a teacher or parent has been angry with you?

The narrator lies to his teacher to protect Amy. He then lies to his mother about what happened at school: who is he now trying to protect? What does his mum's reaction tell you about how well she can care for her son? Who looks after whom? Why do you think his dad left? Why did she get worse, not better, after this?

When he goes out to 'play' he is isolated, alone, apart. He dehumanises the boys he sees drinking, referring to them as 'the two big ones'. His fantasy ends in bloody violence. What do you think really happened? Where would you draw the boundary between reality and fantasy?

Earlier in the story, his mum asked him to stop talking to her, then she frightens him by talking at him, saying things he doesn't understand. What do you think might have been in the empty glass? How do her last words to him connect to the last words of the story? Why is this such a sad and ironic ending?

The narrator is afraid to sleep in his bed, gets drenched on his way to school, is late and his perception of the Lizard King headmaster and the new teacher becomes even more distorted. What does he conclude has happened to Amy? (See if you can find out who the Lizard King is, and what the headmaster's real name might be!)

In the second last paragraph, he again separates himself and goes round to the back of the school. No one notices or cares. His concern is not for himself but for Amy and his mother. Look at how Michael, the writer, uses the sky in the second-last paragraph of the story. What effect does this have?

Michael has also connected the beginning and the end. Compare the very first sentence of the story with the third-last one. What do

you notice? He also uses 'Fire and ice' at both the beginning and the end. At the beginning, he is using it literally, meaning polar ice caps and volcanoes. At the end, he is using fire and ice metaphorically. What is the ice? And the fire?

Did you also notice how Michael uses a *suggestion* of death? In the second paragraph he writes that the mother 'was dead quiet these days', then, during the scary night, 'it was dead quiet' and then at the end of the second-last paragraph, 'I listened to the noise from the playground slowly deaden to silence.' This is clever writing, and gives us subtle clues about the sad ending.

Three masterly techniques used by Michael

1 Having an unusual narrator who sees the world through different eyes.

2 Connecting the beginning to the end by using the same words.

3 Creating characters whose problems drive the narrative.

Your masterpiece

This is a touching and masterly short story exploring the psychological survival mechanism of a solitary young boy who instead of being cared for by parents and teachers, tries to care for his dying mother and attracts only his teacher's anger.

He tries to escape mentally into what he thinks must have been a better place a long time ago when dinosaurs roamed the earth.

Why do you think this was his last day at school?

Write what happens next to him. Can you write a better future for him with more care and love, and less isolation and fewer violent monsters? You can write in the first person, using the same short, simple, childlike sentences as Michael does, or you can write about him from the point of view of the next adult into whose care he comes – his dad? The social services? Someone else? Can you keep the prehistoric connection?

Or:

Write a story in which a child has a problem, and their imagination runs away with them to the point where they confuse reality with fantasy. Can you connect the beginning to the end?

Or:

In both this story and in the next one, 'Jacob's Chicken', a child's drawing is not hung on the wall. How do you think each child feels about this? Write about a time when you either had work accepted or rejected for display. What was it and how did you feel?

Or:

Write in any way you want, using the same title as Michael's story as a starting point.

Jacob's Chicken

Miloš Macourek's Masterpiece

(His name is pronounced **Mill**osh **Mat**so-reck, with the emphasis on the first syllable of each word.)

A chicken is a chicken, you all know how a chicken looks, sure you do, so go ahead and draw a chicken the teacher tells the children, and all the kids suck on crayons and then draw chickens, coloring them black or brown, with black or brown crayons, but wouldn't you know it, look at Jacob, he draws a chicken with every crayon in the box, then borrows some from Laura, and Jacob's chicken ends up with an orange head, blue wings and red thighs and the teacher says that's some bizarre chicken, what do you say children, and the kids roll with laughter while the teacher goes on, saying, that's all because Jacob wasn't paying attention, and, to tell the truth, Jacob's chicken really looks more like a turkey, but then not quite, for it also resembles a sparrow and also a peacock, it's as big as a quail and as lean as a swallow, a peculiar pullet, to say the least, Jacob earns an F for it and the chicken, instead of being hung on the wall, migrates to a pile of misfits on top of the teacher's cabinet, the poor chicken's feelings are hurt, nothing makes it happy about being on top of a teacher's cabinet, so, deciding not to be chicken, it flies off through the open window.

But a chicken is a chicken, a chicken won't fly too far, hence it ends up next door in a garden full of white cherries and powder-blue currants, a splendid garden that proudly shows its cultivator's love, you see, the gardener, Professor Kapon, a recognized authority, is an

$\Rightarrow$

92

ornithologist who has written seven books on birds and right now is finishing his eighth, and as he puts the last touches to it, he suddenly feels weary, so he goes out to do some light gardening and toss a few horseshoes, which is easy and lets him muse over birds, there are tons of them, so many birds, Professor Kapon says to himself, but there isn't a single bird that I discovered, he feels down, flips a horseshoe and dreams a love-filled dream about an as-yet-unknown bird when his eye falls on the chicken picking the baby-blue currants, the rare blue currants that dammit he didn't grow for chicken feed, now that would make anyone's blood boil, the professor is incensed, he is furious, he seems unable to zap the chicken, so in the end he just catches it, flings it over the fence, the chicken flies off, and voilà, Professor Kapon follows, he flies over the fence in pursuit of the chicken, grabs it and carries it home, quite an unusual chicken, that one, bet nobody has seen one quite like it, an orange head, blue wings and red thighs, the professor jots it all down, looks like a turkey, but then not quite, reminds one of a sparrow but also of a peacock, it's as big as a quail and as lean as a swallow, and after he has written it all down for his eighth book, the professor, all quivers, bestows upon the chicken his own name and carries it to the zoo.

A chicken is a chicken, who would fuss over a chicken, you think, but this one must be well worth the bother for the whole zoo is in an uproar, such rarity turns up perhaps once in twenty years, if that often, the zoo director is rubbing his hands, the employees are building a cage, the painter has his hands full and the director says the cage must sparkle and make the bed soft, he adds, and already there appears a nameplate, Kapon's chicken, *Gallina kaponi,* it sounds lovely, doesn't it, what do you say, it sounds, actually, how about it, the chicken is having the time of its life, it's moved to tears by all this care, it really can't complain, it has become the zoo's main attraction, the center of attention, the zoo has never had so many visitors, says the cashier, and the crowds are growing larger by the minute, wait, look, there is our teacher with the whole class standing in front of the cage, explaining, a while ago you saw the Przewalski horse and here you have another unique specimen, the so-called Kapon's chicken or

Gallina kaponi that looks somewhat like a turkey but not quite, resembles a sparrow and also a peacock, it's as big as a quail and as lean as a swallow, why, look at that gorgeous orange head, the blue wings, the scarlet thighs, the children are agog, they sigh, what a beautiful chicken, ain't that right, teacher, but Laura, as if struck by lightning, pulls on teacher's sleeve and says, that's Jacob's chicken, I bet you it is, the teacher becomes irked, this silly child's ridiculous notions, what Jacob's chicken is she prattling about and, come to think of it, where is Jacob anyhow, again he is not paying attention, now, wouldn't you know, there, just look at him, there he is, in front of an anteater's cage, watching an anteater when he is supposed to be looking at Kapon's chicken, Jacob, the teacher yells at the top of her lungs in a high-pitched voice, next time you'll stay home, Jacob, I've had enough aggravation, which shouldn't surprise anyone, for something like that would make anybody's blood boil.

(Translated from the Czech by Dagmar Herrmann)

Questions

Appreciating this masterpiece

This unusual story is, on one level, about a pupil whose teacher fails to recognise his talent. Perhaps you can identify with Jacob?

However, it is also about a much bigger subject that is symbolised by Jacob, his teacher and his chicken. By the time you have answered the following questions you will realise just how masterly a writer Miloš is.

You may have noticed that Miloš has used some techniques here that perhaps your teacher might not normally encourage you to use.

First, let's look at his sentence length and punctuation. What did you notice about the length of Miloš's sentences? And the punctuation of his direct speech?

Remember that this is a professional writer who has made a conscious decision to write this way. Why do you think he chose to do this? What effect has he achieved?

Does it create any problems for you? Why do you think your teachers discourage you from writing like this?

Next, let's look at Miloš's use of repetition.

Look back at the story. What do you notice at the start of each paragraph? What effect do you think this has?

There are three descriptions of Jacob's chicken, one in each paragraph. Look more closely at the *attitude* of each person describing the chicken.

What is the teacher's attitude to the chicken in paragraph 1? What reaction does she want from her class? Quote from this paragraph to support your answer.

What is Professor Kapon's attitude? How does he feel?

And, in the final paragraph, how has the teacher's attitude changed towards the chicken? Quote to support your answer. Can you explain why her attitude has changed so much? Whose chicken does she think it is? Why should this make a difference to her attitude? What does this tell you about what she thinks of Jacob, her inattentive pupil, and of Professor Kapon, 'a recognised authority'?

Let's look now at the main characters that Miloš has created for his story.

We have two adults and two children. What kind of person is the teacher? What do you think of her behaviour towards Jacob both in the classroom and in the zoo?

What kind of person is the professor? He is supposed to be an expert on birds, yet what is his *first* reaction to the chicken? What does this tell you about his ornithological wisdom and knowledge?

Teachers and professors are supposed to be people we can respect for their abilities and learning. What do you think Miloš's attitude to them is? Can you think why he might have this attitude?

Now let's look at Jacob and Laura. What kind of person is Jacob? Why did he not draw a black or brown chicken? How does Laura help him? Laura tries to help him again, at the end of the story. What does she do? Why does the teacher not want to know? What kind of person is Laura?

Now, and this is a big *now*, here is some more information about Miloš Macourek that will shift your perception of this story beyond that of a wee boy and a chicken.

Miloš was Czechoslovakian (he died, aged 75, in 2002). Czechoslovakia was, until the early 1990s, a Communist state. No-one was allowed to openly criticise the ruling regime. There was no democracy, no opposition party, no freedom of speech. The state was the one and only authority.

Writers were not allowed to criticise Communism either. However, Miloš, a masterly writer, created the characters and situation in this story, which he wrote before the fall of Communism, in order to criticise Communism *indirectly*. His characters become symbols, representing something else. 'Jacob's Chicken' is more than a simple story. It is a fable, the purpose of which is to criticise the authoritarian oppression that existed under Communist rule.

What do you think Miloš wants the teacher and the professor to symbolise? What do you think Jacob and Laura symbolise?

Why is the title not quite as simple as it looks?

And what does the chicken itself symbolise? What is the significance of a drawing that comes to life? And the significance of where the chicken ends up? What is Miloš saying about authority figures in a Communist regime? And about freedom and creativity and originality under such a regime?

We have now come a long way from our first reaction to this story which appeared to be only about a teacher judging a child's work harshly.

This extra layer of significance, where the story becomes a secret way of saying something else, makes it *masterly*.

Research on your own

Like a master cabinet-maker decorating his work with ivory inlay, Miloš has embellished his story with some clever little details too. You can still enjoy the story even if you don't appreciate these touches, but if you find out what a 'kapon' is, you will realise just how insulting Miloš is actually being to the professor. (Look up 'capon' because 'kapon' is American spelling. Did you notice any other American spelling? This is because it is an American English, not a British English, translation.)

See if you can find out more about Preswalski's horse too.

What language is 'Gallina kaponi'? What does 'gallina' mean?

See if you can also find out why this language is used in the naming of birds, plants and insects.

Do you know the title of a book by George Orwell, that appears to be a story about animals, but that is also a fable criticising a Communist regime?

Jacob's chicken is multi-coloured. Do you know who else had a coat of many colours? Can you see any connection?

Three masterly techniques used by Miloš

1 Repetition enhanced by a different attitude each time.

2 Conflict.

3 Creating a fable with layers of meaning.

Your masterpiece

This is such a clever and layered story that there are many springboards here for your own writing. Here are a few ideas, and you may, like Jacob, have some of your own.

Please write whatever you feel inspired to write, and use as many colours as you like!

Write about the best or worst teacher you have ever had. It might be wise not to write critically about any teachers you currently have, or if you do want to, then disguise them with false names and false descriptions.

'Surreal' is a French word which means 'beyond-real'. There is a surreal element to this story when the drawing comes to life and turns into a real chicken. Write about another drawing or a photograph, that comes to life. You could use a well-known image, one that appears in this book, a personal one, or an imaginary one.

Or write about what happens next. We have a chicken with the wrong name, caged in a zoo, and a talented young pupil who is magic at drawing...

Or write about a time when someone else wrongly took credit for something you achieved.

There is a lot of anger in and behind Miloš's story. He writes about the teacher's anger with Jacob, both at the beginning and at the end, and about the professor's anger at the chicken eating his rare currants.

Jacob himself might well be angry at the way his teacher treats him, and at seeing the professor taking all the credit for his chicken. The

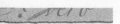

chicken too might become angry. And behind the whole story is Miloš's anger at Communism for stifling creativity.

Write about something that makes you angry. This could be a true piece of autobiography, or a story.

There are many more ways in which you might feel inspired. Here is a sequel written by an English teacher with a lot more imagination than Jacob's teacher. Although she wasn't trying to do a writer's craft task, you can still see where she has picked up on details in the story and where she has added her own characters and events.

Sequel to 'Jacob's Chicken'

Marilyn Copland

'Well, Jacob, how was it for you in school today? It was the zoo visit, wasn't it?'

'Mum, I saw a great thing...'

'Laura's mum said there was some kind of new chicken or something. She said that Laura said YOU knew something about it before you even saw it. Is that right?'

'Mum, that is so passé. A chicken is a chicken. I'm talking about something else...'

'Jacob, take off your jacket. I'm going to put the dinner on the table.'

As his mother turned towards the stove, Jacob clutched his duffel bag by the rope-like fastener and dragged it across the parquet flooring, out of the warm kitchen and across the hall to the room he shared with his grandmother and his younger brother. Under his bed was a huge cardboard box in which he stored his few treasures. He carefully lifted the duffel bag and placed it gently in the box, which he then pushed back to its resting place.

By the time he returned to the kitchen, his grandmother had come in from the allotment with earth-covered potatoes, green beans and rich-coloured beetroot. Alvin, Jacob's brother was also in the room and claimed his mother's attention.

➤

'Mum, mum... the zoo trip was late back. There was "an investigation" the teacher said.'

'A what?'

'"An investigation." One of the beasties went missing.'

As she listened to her younger son, Jacob's mother distractedly but systematically stamped on a line of dark insects which marched across the floor from the sink to the bin, a plague on her house.

Jacob's bright face turned toward his mother.

'Mum, I think I've got the answer to your little problem...'

An Ignorance of Sound

Lesley Sargent's Masterpiece

I bumped into the music maker accidentally one summer's afternoon in the countryside.

A tall man in a long, green overcoat, his haversack filled to bulging with clinking sounds. I was inquisitive, unusually unafraid of his strangeness.

'What are you doing?' I asked directly to his spoon-bowl eyes.

'Collecting,' he replied.

I watched him approach a long-stalked dandelion which he skimmed quickly with a jam jar before slipping on the lid.

'Insects?' I pushed.

'No. Sounds,' he corrected.

I was intrigued and continued to watch him for a further half hour as he stalked the long grass like a crane.

'What kind of sounds?' I ventured as he was about to cork a pretty blue-glass bottle. He frowned at me. 'You've just contaminated the whispering of grass.' He turned the bottle upside down and emptied it into the breeze.

'A person shouldn't speak during these forays,' he said to the horizon. 'The collection must always be pure.'

I apologised. He smiled.

Since there was no objection to my silent presence and I had nothing better to do, I followed him for the rest of the afternoon. I followed him until each of the containers he carried in his haversack had been filled. As he carefully adjusted the straps for comfort he

➤

muttered, 'Tea?' I interpreted this as an economical invitation and responded likewise. 'Where?'

He pointed up the hill with a finger stained from sound. We followed its direction. His home was a tiny cottage with two rooms; one for sleeping, eating and living, the other for the storage of his collection. I sipped my tea with sudden nervousness. In the open this man seemed diluted by the air, but within the confines of that small building his presence began to concentrate. I felt overwhelmed by the strangeness of it all. It became too much to believe, so I left.

For several days afterwards, I found moments to ponder my new acquaintance. All my silences revealed themselves to be simply an ignorance of sound. Now I could hear the things that before I hadn't listened to. The tiniest of noises: a mouse breathing behind the skirting board, a spider spinning its web, a fly eating the sugar. And yet still I could revert to the silence of before and hear nothing. I switched it on. I switched it off.

On realising my newfound skill, I of course rushed to tell. Stumbling over the muddy hoof holes of cows, my meagre torch barely juddered the route into sight. I was disappointed to find he was not at home. Still, this gave me the chance to practise my new talent. Perched on the doorstep, I concentrated my hearing until it found his hand brushing his hair from his eyes. I knew he was nearby, down in the woods capturing the sound of mushrooms pushing up through the soil. By the time he got back, he knew that I knew – I had whispered it into my hand. He said nothing, but I heard his heart skip a beat.

That evening he showed me that there is no such thing as silence. That even objects stationary with dust emit a song. He opened jars together and I heard the symphony of rose petals closing on raindrops, ladybirds singing to unfurling bracken fronds, stones communing with the earth. The last small bottle he opened contained a melody sweet with dew in early morning sunshine and when I asked him what it was, he said it was me.

As I left, he offered a jar into my hand. 'For later,' he said.

I keep it safe, out of direct sunlight, with the lid on. One day when he returns, I will let him out.

Questions

 ## Appreciating this masterpiece

When you read the words 'music maker' in line 1, what kind of person did you expect him to be?

Explain as clearly as you can why the idea in the phrase 'filled to bulging with clinking sounds' is unusual.

Can you also explain why this second sentence isn't, grammatically, a sentence? What one word do you need to add to complete it? Why does its absence not really matter in the context of this story?

Why do you think he speaks 'to the horizon' (lines 18/19)? What does this tell you about how he feels towards the narrator?

What exactly is economical about the invitation and reply in the next, very short paragraph (line 20)? Rewrite both, less economically. Why do you think the music maker speaks like this?

Lesley says his finger was 'stained from sound'. What would be a more realistic substance for his finger to be stained with? Can you suggest what a finger stained with sound might look like, or sound like?

She uses the words 'diluted' and 'concentrate' to describe his presence. In terms of what substance is she describing him? What impact does this have on you?

How has the encounter with this man changed the narrator's life?

Why do you think his heart skips a beat?

Has this story changed, even for a moment, the way you listen?

Consider the tenses Lesley has used. Until the last paragraph, in what tense is the story told? What tense is used in the last paragraph? What effect does this have on the story? (Try missing out the last paragraph to see.)

You too can use this change-of-tense technique at the end of a story for the same effect.

Three masterly techniques used by Lesley

1 Using a surreal idea.
2 Writing with a poetic awareness of the sound of language.
3 Changing the tense to make the ending more effective.

Your masterpiece

There is something about human nature that encourages us to collect. What do you collect now? What have you collected in the past? What do people you know (of all ages) collect?

Can you think of any birds or animals that collect things? What purpose does their collecting have? Is this different in any way from your collecting? Can you think of any official collections? Why do we collect?

Here are two writing ideas for you. The first is non-fiction and is fairly straightforward. The second is much stranger and will test the limits of your creativity.

First, here is an idea for non-fiction. Write about someone you know (or yourself) who collects something. Explain what they collect, giving as much detail as you can about how they acquire and store the objects. Explain why they collect these things and what impact this has on the people around them. Explore the advantages and disadvantages of this particular collection.

Second, here is a stranger idea. Lesley's story is about someone who uses jam jars and a haversack to collect not insects, but sound, which is something that cannot be collected or stored in jars. We can of course collect sounds – we just don't use jam jars for it.

Lesley has combined two senses, sound and touch, by suggesting that we store sound as if it were a physical object like coins or buttons.

Think of something intangible other than sounds. Memories? Emotions? Fears? Keep thinking!

And think of an 'impossible' way of collecting them. Think about how other collections of physical objects are acquired and stored.

Decide who the person doing the collecting is, and why they are doing this. Introduce another character for them to interact with, in either a critical or friendly way.

Now write your own surreal story about an unusual collector.

Fortunately, creative artists have never been held back by the need to be realistic. Often, the best art and writing comes from pushing reality, from having one foot in reality and the other in fantasy. Without this we would have no Hans Christian Andersen, no J. R. R. Tolkien, no J. K. Rowling, no Picasso, no Disney.

Two Wee Mice

Carolyn Mack's Masterpiece

'Down in yonder meadow, where the green grass grows...'

Ah'm the best at ba's. Everybody says so. Ah kin dae wan haunies, scissors an' bridges. An' ah kin talk while ah'm daen them. Ma da says ah kin talk while ah dae anythin'.

Ah canny when ah'm singin' right enough. But if ah'm no singin' ah kin talk and dae the ba's at the same time. Lainy Brady's goat tae stick her tongue oot when she's daen them.

'Where Lizzie Findlay bleaches all her clothes...'

Ah usually get intae trouble for playin' here on Mrs McCann's gable wa'. No' aff ma ma. Aff Mrs McCann.

'Away ye go an' gie's a bit a' peace an' quiet!' she shouts. Ma ma comes oot the windae an' sticks up for me.

'Leave her alane. She's no' daen any herm!' she says. 'At least ah know she's no' at that canal.'

Ah'll no' get intae trouble fur playin' here the day, cos Mrs McCann's no' in. Aw the grown-ups ur away tae chapel fur Danny Williams. We hud tae go yisterday wi' the school. It wis quite good cos we went during sum time. Ah hate sums.

'And she sang and she sang and sang so sweet...'

We hud tae go an' pray fur Danny Williams' soul. Yer soul's inside yer shoulder, but ye cannae see it. If ye've been good it's gold and shiny, an' ye'd need sunglasses to look at it or ye'd go blind. But if ye've been bad it's grey an' dull. Black, if ye've been really bad. Danny Williams

wis bad, that's how we hud tae go an' pray for his soul. Yer soul comes oot yer mooth when ye die an' if it's aw shiny, it goes straight up. But if it's aw black, it starts tae go doon. Ma da says Mrs McCann's soul's definitely gon' doon, but ma ma jist tells him tae wheesht.

If ye want tae keep a soul fae gon' doon everybudy hus tae pray fur it. Like blowin' oan a feather tae keep it up in the air. Then the soul'll go up, up, up so far. But if ye stoap prayin', or ye laugh when ye're prayin' like Peter Dolan did yisterday, the soul'll start comin' doon. Doon, doon, doon til it gets tae Hell an' then it kin never get up again.

Danny Williams should be aboot haufwey up noo. Aboot as high as oor buildin'.

> *'That she sang Danny Williams across her knee.*
> *Lizzie made a dumpling, she made it awfy nice.*
> *She cut it up and slices and gave us all a slice,*
> *Saying taste it, taste it, don't say no,*
> *For tomorrow is our wedding day and I must go.'*

Ah kin sing Danny Williams noo, naebudy'll laugh an' say ah fancy him. Cos he's deid. It's a sin tae laugh at deid people. Yer soul'l go black. John Brady's soul'll be black, as well, cos it wis aw his fault. Even though ma ma said last night it wis his da, Mr Brady's, fault. Ah canny understaun it cos Mr Brady wisnae even there. But ah heard her sayin' it tae ma da:

'See whit Brady's belt an' buckle huv done?'

She said it loud like they wir arguin' even though he hudny said anythin'.

> *'One, two, buckle my shoe;*
> *three, four, knock on the door...'*

This is a hard wan tae play cos ye've goat tae dae the actions as well.

Mr Brady hits his weans wi' a belt, sometimes wi' the buckle if they've been really bad. Wan time Lainy showed me a big mark oan her back, jist up fae her bum, where her da hud whacked her wi' the buckle. It wis the time we got caught up at the canal.

Ma ma didnae hit me fur it. She jist hud that look oan her face. The wan that makes me aw horrible inside, an' she jist said tae me:

'Lizzie, ah thoat ye knew better.'

Jist that. That wis aw. Lainy Brady said ah wis lucky. But, ah didnae feel very lucky.

'Five, six, pick up sticks…'

He hits them wi' sticks as well. Anythin' that's lyin' aroon'.

'It's no' right,' ma ma says tae ma da. 'Ah'm gonny report him wan ae these days.'

But he jist says it's nane ae oor business.

Mr Brady's a bad man awright, but he didnae hit Danny Williams so ah don't know how ma ma kin blame him fur it. Ah asked ma da but he jist patted ma heid an' said ah'm too wee tae understaun.

'Seven, eight, shut the gate…'

There's a gate at the canal, but some ae the big boays huv dug the dirt underneath so ye kin get in if ye crawl really low. That's where ah wis when ah got caught, haufwey underneath. Lainy wis already through, then we wur gettin' shouted fur wur tea an' ma ma saw me fae the windae.

Everybody gets shouted fur their tea at five roon here. Windaes go up an' wummin are oot oan the streets shouting, 'Lizzie!' 'Lainy!' 'John!' 'Danny!'

That's aw ye hear at five a'clock. Ma da says when he wins the pools he's gonny buy aw the weans bloody watches. Ma ma jist tells him tae wheesht.

'The night was dark and the war was over,
The battlefield all covered in blood…'

This wan's awful sad, aboot a soldier gettin' killed. Ah always get a lump in ma throat when ah sing it.

Danny Williams' ma wis gonny kill him the other night. No' really kill him like. It's jist wan ae thae things yer ma says. Everybudy wis gettin' shouted fur their tea. Then everybudy went in. The windaes went doon, the doors shut an' it wis aw quiet, except fur Mrs Williams:

'Danny… Danny… DANNY!'

Her voice wis gettin' louder when ma ma opened the windae an' shouted:

'Kin ye no' find him, Betty?'

'Naw. Ah'll kill him when ah dae.'

'Haud oan an ah'll send Jimmy doon tae gie ye a haun',' ma ma said.

Ma da rolled his eyes up, but ah knew he didnae really mind. Ma ma pit the rest ae his dinner in the oven. While ah wis eatin' mine ah' tried tae count every time ah heard ma da shoutin' oan Danny.

But then there wis too many voices shouting. Men and wummin. The shoutin' wis gettin' louder. Then people started chappin' the door askin' if we hud seen Danny an' ma ma wid tell them that ma da wis oot lookin' fur him tae.

> 'There I spied a wounded soldier,
> lying, dying, saying these words...'

Ah knew Danny wis in big trouble noo. Ma ma an' da huv hud tae come oot an' look fur me a couple a' times, but never the whole street!

It wis nine a'clock when ma da came up fur a heat an' a cup a tea. He kept runnin' his hauns through his herr. He always does that when he's worried aboot somethin'. He told ma ma tae keep his dinner in the oven.

He asked me if ah'd seen Danny in school that day an' if he'd said he wis gon' anywhere. Ah hud tae think. Aw schooldays seem the same tae me. The bell rings, then ye're in class, say prayers, dae sums, dae spelling . . . Then ah remembered that John Brady hud broke ma good pencil at hame time. Ah didnae tell anybudy because ma ma disnae like me telling oan the Bradys, no' even tae the teacher. Danny Williams hud tried tae fix it fur me but it wis snapped right in two.

Ah told him the last time ah seen Danny and John they were running up tae the canal gate.

'But John says he's no' seen him since school,' ma da said as if he didnae believe me.

> 'God bless my home in bonny bonny Scotland,
> Bless my wife and my only child...'

Then he tells ma ma they're callin' the polis, an' she says, 'Oh, dear God!'

But ah don't think she wis prayin'.

She goat gloves an' a scarf fur ma da cos it wis gettin' really cauld noo an' he went away back oot.

The shoutin' stoapped when the polis came. Three motors an' a big van parked oan the sper grun acroass fae us. We could see everythin'. People stopped lookin' an' gathered roon them. Fur a minute ah thoat they wur gonny pull Danny oot a motor, like a magic trick. But aw they did wis gie oot torches an' whistles.

Mrs McCann came up tae tell ma ma that some ae the big boays hud beat up auld Sandy Patterson, jist because he lived hisel' and gave the weans ginger boattles. Ma ma shook her heid an' said, 'Oh, merciful God. They're no' helpin' anybody, cerryin' oan like that.'

She forgoat tae tell me it wis bedtime. She opened the windae, even though it wis frosty, and an' told me tae listen fur a whistle 'cos when somebody blew their whistle it meant they'd found Danny.

A wee while later we smelt somethin' burnin'. Ma ma ran tae the oven, but she wis too late. Ma da's dinner wis burnt black. She started greetin'. No' loud or anythin', jist quiet like, tae herself. Ah couldnae understaun it! She only greets at sad films, or if she hears somethin' bad. She never greets aboot burnt dinners an' stuff.

Ah didnae like her greetin' so ah showed her ma trick. Haudin' a pencil like a fag an' blowin' my breath oot the windae like smoke. She nodded an' smiled, but she wisnae lookin' at me, she wis lookin' oot at the canal.

Ah didnae really care cos ah wis getting' tae stey up late.

> '*God bless this earth which I lie under,*
> *Holding up St Andrew's flag...*'

We never heard any whistles. We could hardly even hear the shoutin'. Jist far away. Wan time ah heard somebody shoutin', 'Mammy', an' ah thoat Danny wis back.

But ma ma leaned oot the windae an' said it was 'Danny' they were shoutin'.

Ma da came back at eleven fur merr tea. He hud lost his gloves lookin' through the middens. His hauns wur blue wi' the cauld an' aw cut, but he didnae care. He wis tryin' tae tell ma ma somethin' in secret.

Ah kin always tell. Like when it's ma birthday or Christmas or somethin'. Ah kin see his lips movin'. Ah seen somethin' aboot 'draggin' the canal' an' 'a big machine tae brek the ice'. Ma ma just sat doon an' put her heid in her hauns an' said, 'Naw. That poor wee boay.'

> *'Two wee mice went skating on the ice,*
> *Singing pollywally doodle all the day…'*

Fur wans ah wis gled we lived three sterrs up. Ah could see right err tae the canal bank. They hud opened the big gates an' everybody wis there. Big lights went oan an' ah see could real frogmen, like in *Flipper* oan the telly. When the noise fae the big machine started ma ma shut the windae. She went an' sat at the fire an' kept tellin' me tae come away fae the windae. But ah wanted tae see wit wis happenin'. When ah turned roon she hud her rosary beads oot. She always gets them oot fur good luck when somethin's wrang.

Ah must huv fell asleep cos the next thing ah remember is seein' the rosary beads burnin' oan the fire. Ah grabbed the poker an' tried tae get them oot. But ma ma jist said tae leave them an' go tae bed.

> *'But the ice was thin and one fell in…'*

Peter Dolan says he seen Danny gettin' pult oot the canal. He says he came oot feet furst, an' he wis aw eaten away wi' the rats.

He's a liar, but. Ma da says Danny jist looked as if he wis sleepin'.

'Too cauld fur the rats, hen,' he said. 'Too bloody cauld…'

John Brady's soul'll be black noo, fur no' tellin' aboot Danny. Peter Dolan says he'll get sent tae jail!

He jist ran away an' never told anybudy when Danny fell through the ice. Went hame an' kidded on nothin' hud happened. He wis too feart tae tell he hud been up the canal.

Ma ma seen Mr Brady yesterday. That's when she said, 'See whit Brady's belt an' buckle huv done?'

Ma da never answered her.

Then she shook her heid an' said, 'God help us aw. That poor wee boay.'

But she wis getting' aw mixed up, cos she wis lookin' err at John Brady's hoose when she said it.

> *'Singing, mammy, daddy, help me, ah'm away.*
> *CLOSE YOUR EYES!'*

Questions

 ## Appreciating this masterpiece

This is one of two short stories by Carolyn Mack which were both judged among the top 20 from over 2000 anonymous entries in a national competition, the Macallan/Scotland on Sunday Short Story Prize.

Did you enjoy it? Do you think it is good? Why?

What is the story about? What has happened? Why has Danny William's life not been saved?

Carolyn has created a persona to narrate this story. Who is narrating the story? What is she doing at the same time?

How did the narrator feel about Danny Williams? How do you know?

What is the first thing you notice about the typography and layout?

What do you notice about the registers of the two different typographical styles, that is, the parts in normal typestyle and the parts in italics?

From what genre of writing is the first line? How do you know? There are two words in the first line that we would not use now: translate them into their modern equivalent. Why does it not work so well? You might like to think about syllables and rhythm.

Can you see any connection developing between the songs and the story itself?

Most of the words in this story will be well known to you, although they have been deliberately spelt differently. What effect has Carolyn achieved with this? If you're not sure about this, try rewriting the first two paragraphs in standard English. The result might surprise you!

When do you think this story is set? Where do you think it is set? How do you know?

The structure of the story is not chronological, that is, it is not told in the order in which events happen because we know early on that Danny Williams is dead. Why do we still read on? What does this tell you about suspense and about ways of ordering stories?

At the end, the narrator, the persona of the wee girl, is still puzzled. She thinks her mother is getting mixed up. In fact, Carolyn is doing

a masterly thing here, because she makes her narrator give us enough information to enable us to understand why her mother is looking over at John Brady's house with pity. Carolyn has created two layers of storytelling here. The first is the story told in the persona of the wee girl, and the second is the one we can deduce beyond that. You can also find masterly (but different) layers of storytelling in 'Jacob's Chicken' on page 92.

As you've probably realised, this story hasn't happened by accident. It has been carefully crafted. There are several elements that Carolyn has planted casually early on in the story which come back with much more importance later on. Look at where she has first used the following four elements: Lainy Brady, the canal, shouting and windows. They seem unimportant at first, but how are these four elements used, some of them several times, later in the story?

Do you find any humour in the story? What is funny and why? Why do we need humour in a tragic story?

Carolyn's inspiration

Carolyn remembers a wee boy drowning in the canal at Maryhill, in Glasgow, near where she lived. She was about five at the time and he would have been about four. Some people said his pal ran away, others that his pal or a man tried to save him.

More recently, there was another tragedy on the same canal. A four-year-old and a six-year-old boy were playing on the ice. The four-year-old fell in, then the six-year-old, trying to help, also fell in. Someone ran for their grandpa from the pub. He too fell in and all three were drowned.

Carolyn also remembers the first wee boy's mother at his funeral. Carolyn was standing on the pavement and his mother was walking behind the hearse, grief-stricken. When she saw Carolyn, she reached out to her, as a mother who had lost her own child. But, all in black and weeping, she was also a bit frightening.

These are the truths that inspired Carolyn. But as they stand, they don't fit neatly into a story. Can you see what Carolyn has changed, has added, has missed out, from the realities in order to create both her story and her storyteller?

This is how the best writers work. They start with realities and they change them: they add bits, they remove bits, they make connections, they create characters, they make patterns with words

and ideas. It's not easy and it takes time, but it's worth it for the sense of satisfaction that can come from having crafted something (anything!) well.

What Carolyn likes best about her story is the detached way that the child is telling it. She is playing a game at the same time and she seems unaffected by the tragedy of the drowned child although, ironically, the sad song about the soldier getting killed does affect her. Look back at this bit now, page 107, if you don't remember it.

Three masterly techniques used by Carolyn

1 Linking fragments of songs with the story.
2 Using two different registers.
3 Managing to spell in a way that lets us 'hear' the Glaswegian dialect and accent as we read it.

Your masterpiece

In Carolyn's story, the children had been forbidden from playing at the canal.

Think of somewhere dangerous where you were forbidden to play when you were younger, or where you are forbidden to play now. Write a story about something that happens in such a place.

Before you start, decide whether you want to tell the story from the distance of third person, or whether you want to adopt the persona of a first person narrator as Carolyn has done here, or you might want to write it as autobiography. Perhaps you can think of songs or nursery rhymes that you too could weave into your story? (This will take some planning and hard thinking and you might want to research songs or rhymes in other books.)

Or:

Songs and music are important to us and are often associated with powerful memories. If you prefer to do a personal piece of writing, choose a song or a piece of music that is important to you or to someone you know. Write about it, telling us as much as you can about the song, why it matters, to whom it matters and what effect it has.

The Myths of Childhood Uncovered

Laura J. Rennie's First Masterpiece

The older one gets, the greater the disenchantment. The other day, I was 'winding up' my small younger cousin, and it made me think back to the earlier days of my own youth, back to the days when what older, wiser people said to me really meant something, when they spoke only the gospel truth, when I really truly believed them, when my big brother said to me, whilst I was eating an apple: 'Laura, if you swallow any of those apple pips, they'll lie in your tummy, and all the food that you eat will fall on top of it, an' that'll be like soil, an' a plant'll grow, an' that'll turn into a tree, and the tree will grow hundreds of feet tall, an' the branches will pop out of your nose and your ears, and you'll turn into a tree, and if you don't die, Dad'll plant you in the garden, and all the birds will peck your eyes and do the toilet on you.'

Now my brother, who was 13, and me, who was 4 at the time, got on rather well until he came out with things like that which made me go screaming to my mother. (I'd remembered that earlier that day I had consumed a bag of grapes, seeds and all.) I know that adults tell children slight fabrications to make life easier, like, how Wee Willie Winkie will get you into trouble if you weren't in bed on time and stories about the Sandman and stuff, but Buddy used to tell me that there was a Troll living under my bed, and that he spoke to it, and that its favourite food was little girls. How convenient.

Bedtime for me became a heart-racing ritual. After my bath, which I used to love, but began to detest since I learned that Trolls love clean little girls more than just ordinary ones, I would enter my room,

115

silently opening the door. Stealthily, I would sneak to the light switch and flick it off. The orangey glow of the outside streetlamp made the shadow of the tree outside my window dance along the wall, and my heart miss a beat. Next came a manoeuvre that would result in life or death. I would hold my breath, (because Trolls can locate you if they hear you breathing), and leap over the rug that separated me from the safety of my bed.

Here, I feel that I should explain some points about escaping Trolls. If you land on the bed with one foot dangling over, then you've had it. The Troll comes and gets you the next night when you're sleeping and takes you to Trolldom, where you get turned into a tree, and Troll birds do the toilet on you forever. If you land with both feet on the duvet, then you're safe, only if you can get under the covers before you breathe out.

I was quite a worried child, what with avoiding Trolls and having to be in bed before some wee chap starts staring through the window from outside, so I was quite relieved when Bud came in to see if I was comfortable and ready to sleep.

'Laura?' he whispered as he crouched down beside my bed.
'What?'
'I wouldn't go to sleep if I was you...'
'Why not?'
'Well, you know about the Sandman, don't you?'
'Uh-huh...'
'Well, it's all lies.'
'What do you mean?'
'Well, it's not true that he sprinkles sand in your eyes.'
'What does he do then, Bud?'
'He super-glues your eyelids shut when you're asleep. G'night!'
'... MUUUUM!!'

It took me a few years of insomnia before a close friend noticed my strange nocturnal habits and questioned them one night, whilst staying over. I was sat down, and gently told that Trolls and glue-wielding Sandmen didn't exist.

The enchanted Troll kingdom under my bed vanished. The vision of the little man with the tube of glue peering in my window crumbled, and instead of feeling relieved, I felt sort of sad. It took me ages to get used to breathing at bedtime, and closing my eyes and actually getting to sleep easily, and even my mum missed the thud of me landing on my bed.

It's funny, because when I think back to it, I remember how much it affected my life then, even though it's the last thing on my mind at the present time.

Thanks to Buddy, I developed a long stride at the age of seven, as well as a fear of multi-coloured carpets. Let me explain.

Whenever we went out together, and where the pavement was made up of concrete slabs, Bud would say that I would have to walk over all the lines where the squares met... one step per square, and if my foot touched a line, I would become The Devil's Pet. As my legs were not as long as my lanky brother's, I would frequently fall victim to the repetitive taunt of 'Devil's Pet, Devil's Pet...'

He still notices if I step on a line, and he still taunts me, and he's 25!

Anyway, I became quite upset at his jibes, and demanded a piggy back to avoid any more contact with the ground. This was all great until we got home and into the living room which had a carpet of multi-coloured swirls swirling into each other, occasionally splashed with a dot of black. He told me that the coloured bits were shark-infested waters, and that he was going to drop me. I was, to say the least, petrified, and my Dad's convincing 'shark sightings' and calls of, 'There's one! Behind the chair!' didn't help. My parents were safe on couch island, and Buddy just happened to be wearing shark-proof boots. He released his grip and I was left dangling from his neck, howling. Thankfully my Mum informed me that the black blotches on the carpet were stepping stones, so I dropped onto one, and leapt onto the couch, screaming at the cat to get off the carpet. I thought I'd got over it, but I still find myself responding when Buddy says, 'I bet you can't make me a cup of tea before I count to ten. One... two...' You can't see me for dust!

I catch myself setting little goals, like, I have to get a can of Coke from the fridge and make a sandwich during the adverts of a programme and get back in to watch it before it comes back on, or else a monster will jump out of a cupboard and eat me.

Maybe my brother was sick to me, but he's given me a whole new outlook on life, to not take stuff so seriously, and not to worry too much. He made my younger years incredibly exciting, like an adventure, and in a way, I miss that, but now, I just see life as a big adventure, and I'm ready for what's next, Trolls and all... (But now I only eat seedless grapes...)

Questions

 ## Appreciating this masterpiece

Have you worked out how old (or young) Laura was when she wrote this? There are enough clues in the story for you to do this!

Do you agree with the first sentence? Say why, or why not? Did you have an enchanted childhood?

Contrast the length of this first sentence with the second one. How many times does Laura deliberately repeat 'when'? What effect does she create with this repetition?

Comment both on the *way* her brother, Buddy, speaks and on *what* he says. What impact does this have on the reader?

How does Laura's style change in the second paragraph? Comment on sentence length and pace in both paragraphs.

Can you find two complex words she uses that indicate that this is the register of a young adult and not a child writing? Can you think of simpler, more childlike words instead?

Laura writes, 'How convenient.' at the end of paragraph 2. What is the tone of this sentence? Why does its length give it such impact?

'Silently... stealthily... sneak... flick...' (paragraph 3) how does Laura's choice of these particular words give this part more impact?

Try removing them and replacing them with less precise words to see the difference. What literary device is she also using here?

Look at paragraph 4. What does Laura achieve by using 'you', the second person, here instead of 'I/me', the first person?

Laura reveals a lovely light sense of humour when she writes about life after Trolls in the paragraph beginning, 'The enchanted Troll kingdom under my bed vanished…'. Why do you think there was also a sense of loss?

Both of Laura's parents go along with Buddy's shark-infested carpet fantasy but they each side with a different child. In what way does her dad side with Buddy, and how does her mother side with Laura? Who or what does Laura care most about?

What two remarks does Laura make at the end that suggest perhaps she hasn't quite left her brother's influence behind?

Three masterly techniques used by Laura

1 Using conflict in several ways.
2 Including dialogue.
3 Endearing us to her by making fun of herself.

Your masterpiece

We have all, surely, been afraid of mythical creatures when we were young.

Here's your big opportunity to put your own childhood fears on record! Write about something imaginary, or mythical, that *you* were afraid of when you were small. See if you can explore why you were scared or even perhaps who put these fears into your head. How did your family react to your fears? How did you get over them, or have they had a lasting impact?

Remember that if you don't mind making fun of yourself and revealing weakness, then your readers will find it much easier to identify with your writing. The opposite is true too: if a writer comes over as knowing everything and being very arrogant too, then we don't like them any more on the page than we would in real life.

Try to use Laura's masterly technique of drawing in the reader by using 'you' sometimes, instead of 'I'. It can be very effective. You might also want to illustrate this autobiographical piece!

Or, if you were a fearless child, write instead about a brother or sister or friend with whom there was some conflict when you were younger.

My One True Friend

Laura J. Rennie's Second Masterpiece

It was autumn. The air was crisp and fresh. We were standing on the underground platform, my Dad and I.

Down at the end of the station sat a medium sized mongrel, just beyond puppyhood, laughing. Her eyes glowed with a tremendous good nature and trust. She was alone.

'Hello,' I said. She came over, licked my hand discreetly, allowed my Dad to scratch her for a while, chased her tail in a dignified circle and lay down again. I remember my Dad saying, 'There are times when God puts a choice in front of you.'

She went totally mad when she understood, bounding and leaping to kiss my face. To get her home in one piece, I had to hold her like a baby. It's a silly position for a dog, and most fight it. Not her. She lay in my arms, feet poking skyward, head lolling back in a friendly grin, tongue draping out of the corner of her mouth, eyes calmly investigating mine as if to say, 'This is a good idea. Why didn't you think of it before?'

We named the dog Tessa. Height about 30 inches. Weight, 35 pounds. Eyes, brown. Tongue, red, and a coat of pure china white, thick, lustrous and profuse. In the winter she shed badly, and worse in the summer. All my clothes were covered in a fine layer of white flax as was the furniture, much to the dismay of my mum and her hoover.

When she was young, her tummy was as pink as a baby's bottom, and she had a marvelous puppy smell, clean, pungent, yet sweet. Her personality? All I can say is that when she was made, God forgot to

➤

121

add any malice, guile or aggression. She didn't even chase squirrels. If another dog attacked her, she would immediately roll over on her back and expose her soft underbelly, clearly conveying the message: 'Go ahead and kill me. I don't mind, but I think it would be an unnecessary waste of energy. That's just my opinion though.'

Not once in her life was she hurt by any living creature.

Tessa was not clever, but she made the most of it. 'She's the sweetest dog in the world,' said a friend, 'But she's got an IQ somewhere between that of a brick and a houseplant.' To all intents and purposes, she was also mute: not a bark, yelp or whimper escaped her. In 12 years I heard her voice maybe three times. It was always a shock.

After a while, our house became a dog's house, which I suppose was only fair. Empty tins of her dog food littered the kitchen bin and squeaky bones and other toys lay scattered about the floor, and long skeins of toilet paper hung everywhere, for when Tess got bored she loved to play with it. She tore into rubbish bags and distributed the contents. She kept herself occupied.

Tess loved to run. I would take her to the park, and she would sprint in a circle until I thought her heart would burst from exertion and joy. If we piled her in the back of Dad's car she'd sleep, and shed, but that was okay, it was a dog's car too. Tess was a perfect example of how a dog should adjust to urban living. When we returned from walks I'd let her off the leash at the end of our street and she'd tear off like a hound possessed, her tail tucked under her rear end for maximum aerodynamic lift and thrust, slam into the wall at the end, turn and head back at even greater speed.

She was youth and spirit and careless vitality. When we went to the seaside for day trips, she was there, zipping freely down the beach, chasing the waves until they crashed over her and Dad had to rescue her from the undertow.

One night, we went home to a meal of noodles and chicken, and Mum put the salad on the floor as the table was full. As we talked in the dimmed light, we heard a moist chomping noise and a great smacking of lips. We looked beneath the table, and it was Tess,

downing the last of the goat's cheese and tomatoes. She looked up at us, the vinaigrette glistening off her whiskers, as if to say, 'This is delicious, but how about some of that chicken to wash it down?'

Tess took the occasional visits of my two younger cousins with grace, even when they fell on her, pulling her eyebrows or screaming and hugging and kissing her. When one of my cousins was three, and particularly aggressive, he tried to ride on her back. She was 10 by then and growled at him.

One morning, two years ago, Tessa couldn't get up. We took her to the vet, who told us that her spleen was enlarged. Would we care to make a decision? After all, the dog was 12. We patched her up. While she was convalescing at the surgery, my sister confided in me that she was really missing Tess. We both cried. How much is a dog's life worth?

The following Tuesday, after breakfast, Tess fell down and just lay there, her eyes rolled up into her skull, heaving and panting and trembling. The episode lasted just a few minutes, but it scared me. When she awoke, she was jolly and hungry, and spent the rest of the day staring off into space, one of her favourite pastimes.

When she was falling down five times a day, the vet said to us, 'You have to decide whether she is able to preserve her dignity leading this type of existence.' I'd never considered it in those terms.

'Take her home for the weekend and love her,' the vet told me.

As she lay on her side, clearly not in this world, I held her paw and kissed her forehead and all the 12 years of my life with her swam before me, and I knew. It was not a good knowing. My Dad gently wrapped her back up in her blanket and placed her in the back of the car with me.

The vet's surgery was clean and cool. He's a nice fellow, my vet. I got the feeling that he'd never get used to this part of his job. 'The first shot will put her to sleep easily,' he said. 'The next shot will put her to rest.' I held her, sobbing, as my mum looked on, and the vet said a few minutes later, 'She's at peace now.' He was weeping too.

Tessa's body was there, the coat still shiny, the nose still wet and warm, and her tongue hanging out much as it had been the very first day I saw her. But she was gone.

This is the last I will say of her.

I owe her this eulogy, for 12 years of companionship, of laughs and devotion and cheek-by-jowl existence on this hard and incomprehensible planet.

You were the best. The kindest.

The last who was wholly mine.

Bye, girl.

Questions

 ### Appreciating this masterpiece

Comment on the effect achieved by Laura's use of short sentences in the first two paragraphs.

Why is 'laughing' in paragraph 2, both unusual and appropriate as a description for Tessa?

Laura gives us lots of happy pictures of Tessa in action. Which three are the most memorable for you, and what do they reveal about Tessa's personality?

Reread the two paragraphs starting at, 'After a while, our house became…'. Find two unusual humorous expressions that Laura uses to show just how much Tessa has taken over their lives. Why are these funny?

There are always both good and less good aspects to owning any pet. What are three less good aspects of living with Tessa?

The first two thirds of this tribute are happy memories, a celebration of Tessa's good years. Which short sentence signals the turning point from happiness to the beginning of the end?

When the vet says, 'You have to decide whether she is able to preserve her dignity leading this type of existence', Laura writes that she had never considered it in those terms. What does she mean? What terms had she been considering it in?

Laura describes Tessa's end (she never uses the word 'death' or 'dead' – why not?) in a way that affects us emotionally. Partly this is because through her writing, we have come to know Tessa too; partly because we can all identify with the loss, or the thought of

loss, of a beloved pet; and partly because of the powerful impact of her short simple sentences, each with an emotionally charged unit of information.

What do you think it is for Laura that makes this planet 'hard and incomprehensible'? What comforting thoughts can you think of for such a time? Do you think that writing this would have made Laura feel better or worse? Why?

Three masterly techniques used by Laura

1 Using powerful emotions as inspiration.

2 Jump cutting (see below) to maintain good pace.

3 Creating a character using detailed description, actions and places.

Jump cutting

This is a term used in the editing of films or television programmes. A jump cut is when there is a cut and the action 'jumps' forwards significantly in the next shot. We can also use it in writing.

Here is the last sentence of paragraph 3 and the first sentence of paragraph 4.

> ...I remember my Dad saying, 'There are times when God puts a choice in front of you.'
>
> She went totally mad when she understood...

There is a unit of information that Laura has decided not to tell us, which is, that between paragraphs 3 and 4, she makes her choice. This is a jump cut. Confident writers know that they can miss out some information and that their readers are clever enough still to understand. So Laura didn't need to say, 'I decided to keep her and dad said it was OK.'

This masterly technique makes your writing less predictable and gives it a better pace. (See page 26 for more information about pace.) It is not something we are often conscious of, but, at the editing stage, you can go back over your writing and see how important each piece of information is.

For example, here are four sentences:

> I needed a new tyre for my bike. So I got my money, went down to the shops and bought one. I carried it back home.
>
> When Dad came home later, he was really pleased to see that I'd manage to fit it all by myself.

Here, you could miss out the middle two sentences because they don't add anything we can't deduce from the last sentence, and there is nothing eventful about going to the shop, buying a tyre, bringing it home and fitting it.

However, if the child had bought the wrong size of tyre, or had wrecked it when he was trying to fit it, then those pieces of information would be needed.

If you edit your content deliberately, including only necessary information, then your writing will be more effective.

Your masterpiece

There is a very simple chronological structure to this tribute to Tessa. It begins with her arrival in Laura's life and ends with her death.

Laura writes, 'There are times when God puts a choice in front of you'.

Think of a time when you, or someone you know, had a life-changing choice. It could be a choice about doing or not doing something, saying or not saying something, going or not going somewhere, accepting or rejecting something or someone. Write about the consequences of this choice. (See if you can use a jump cut or two. You might find it easier to do this at the redrafting stage.)

Or:

Our relationships with the other living creatures in our lives is special and very different from our relationships with people. Write a tribute to an animal or bird that shares, or has shared your life. Make notes of events or incidents that reveal the character and personality of this creature, and try to explain why you love them. Again, use a jump cut or two if you can.

No More Birthdays & Deformed Finger

Hal Sirowitz's Masterpieces

Read each of these poems at least twice before you think about the following questions.

No More Birthdays

Don't swing the umbrella in the store,
Mother said. There are all these glass jars
of spaghetti sauce above your head
that can fall on you, & you can die.
Then you won't be able to go to tonight's party,
or go to the bowling alley tomorrow.
And instead of celebrating your birthday
with soda & cake, we'll have
anniversaries of your death with tea
& crackers. And your father & I won't
be able to eat spaghetti anymore, because
the marinara sauce will remind us of you.

Deformed Finger

Don't stick your finger in the ketchup bottle,
Mother said. It might get stuck, &
then you'll have to wait for your father
to get home and pull it out. He
won't be happy to find a dirty fingernail
squirming in the ketchup that he's going to use
on his hamburger. He'll yank it out so hard
that for the rest of your life you won't
be able to wear a ring on that finger.
And if you ever get a girlfriend, &
you hold hands, she's bound to ask you
why one of your fingers is deformed,
& you'll be obligated to tell her how
you didn't listen to your mother, &
insisted on playing with a ketchup bottle
& she'll get to thinking, he probably won't
listen to me either, & she'll push your hand away.

Questions

Appreciating these masterpieces

What nationality do you think this poet is? Can you quote at least
three words as evidence? Can you think of three other words that a
writer from this country might use that are different from yours?

You will notice that there is a similar pattern to these poems. Look
at the first two lines of each poem. What pattern do you notice in
the words? What pattern do you notice in the content of each
poem?

How badly behaved do you think the wee boy is? What age do you
think he is? Why?

Look at the chain of events that the mother predicts. What is the
worst thing that might happen in each poem?

What does the ending of the first poem, 'No More Birthdays', tell you about how the mother feels towards her son? Think carefully about this – what is it that matters most to her?

Why do you think the writer uses the word 'Mother' rather than Mummy, Mum, Ma or Mom? What is he telling you about his relationship with his mother? How does the register of 'mother' differ from the other forms of address? In what contexts might you use these other forms?

What kind of character is the mother? How do you think she feels towards her son? How do we know?

How much does Hal characterise the wee boy? What kind of character do you think he is? How do you think he feels? Do we have any evidence from the poems for this?

Do you think these poems are funny? Do you think Hal wants you to find them funny?

Some people might argue that these poems are not very poetic. They don't rhyme and they don't use literary techniques like simile or alliteration. How could you persuade someone that they are poems? You might like to consider the shape on the page, the rhythms they do have and the pace at which you need to read them, bearing in mind the distance, in terms of ideas, that each poem travels between the first and last line.

What do you notice about the ways Hal uses the conjunction 'and' (the word) and '&' (the ampersand sign)? Can you work out what 'rule' he is applying? Why do you think he does this? (There is more information for you about ampersands on page 131.)

What do you notice about sentence length, and sentence structure? Do Hal's sentences become more or less complex? Why do you think they change?

Three masterly techniques used by Hal

1 Exaggeration.
2 Using conflict between an adult and a child for black humour.
3 Creating a very strong, unusual character.

Your masterpiece

Psychologists are people who study how our minds work and how we behave. They have a word for the way this mother's mind works:

it's called 'catastrophising'. 'Catastrophe' is another word for disaster, and someone who 'catastrophises' turns tiny little things into the worst possible endings. So, for example, if someone is late home, their thoughts of disasters will run away with them until they think the only possible explanation is that the person must be kidnapped or dead.

Hal Sirowitz has used this psychological process here. You can too!

Think of a very small thing that a parent or teacher might not want a child to do. See if you can list five different things.

Choose one to develop and see if you can come up with three or four increasingly awful consequences, ending up with the worst catastrophe you can think of. This is all about exaggeration!

Then, using Hal's poems as a model, write your own poem. Start your first and second lines the same way as Hal does, using Father or Teacher, if you prefer.

You can write more than one poem if you enjoy it.

Ampersands

Ampersand is the big word for this little sign: &.

It is a shorter way of saying 'and', not normally used in books. Where would you expect to find it? Why? Look around the world on your way home and see if you can spot any ampersands.

The ampersand is a combination (or ligature) of the two letters 'e' and 't', making the word 'et', which is Latin (and French) for 'and'. (Can you see the two letters?)

You may have come across 'et' already in 'etc'. This is short for 'et cetera' which, in Latin, means 'and other things'.

If you know this, then you won't make the common mistake of writing 'ect' instead of 'etc'.

Can you think of any other symbols (or monograms) that are a combination of more than one letter? Can you design a monogram of your own initials?

Loving & Loathing
DIY Masterpieces

Here is a process that will result in you writing a powerful poem with ease!

There are several stages in this process, including brainstorming and making careful editorial choices, but at the end of it, you will be impressed by what you and your fellow pupils have achieved. You will also see at first hand the impact of simile and metaphor.

1 Make sure you have two separate sheets of lined paper.

2 Jacket, trousers, scarf – what category do these three items belong to? Write down the one-word answer next to the left-hand margin on the first line of your first sheet of paper. Tractor, car, lorry – what category do these three items belong to? Again, write down the answer on the line below your first category. See if you can come up with other groups of three for your classmates to guess the categories. Write down each category below the previous one. Continue until you have a list of between 15 and 20 categories down the left-hand side of your page. (Flute, guitar, piano? Rain, snow, sunshine? Flu, cholera, pneumonia?)

3 Now think of someone you really like or really loath. It can be someone you know well, or a public figure. If it's someone you can't stand, you should avoid using anyone who is in your class!

Once you have decided, go back to your list of categories. Next, you will have to use your imagination, just a little bit...

Let's say you've chosen someone you detest, and let's say the first item on your list is clothes. Imagine what this person would *be* if they *were* that item of clothing!

You might decide they would be socks. But the word 'socks' on its own doesn't indicate whether you love them or loathe them. So you need to use adjectives or short descriptive phrases to make this clear.

So perhaps, 'a smelly old sock full of holes'?

4 Work your way down the full list coming up with a specific item for each category. Don't write in sentences. This is the creative stage and you are only making notes.

Check that it's obvious from each line of notes how you feel about the person. Stick to either loving or loathing all the way through. You can always do a second poem later from the opposite feeling.

You will find some categories much easier than others. Miss out the ones that give you big problems. (Creating is about recognising dead ends as well as good paths to take.) Try to come up with notes for at least ten categories.

5 When you have finished your list (well done!) read the following two poems – aloud if possible – written by P7 pupils:

She is... *Heather Anne McTaggart*

> She is a broken chair
> She is a brown cow
> She is lightening
> She is a scary video
> She is a smelly curry
> She is an old banger
> She is a yellow wet-the-bed

I Hate my Brother *Owen Smith*

I hate my brother
he is like a Skoda – he is unreliable
you drive it for a month
and it breaks down.

He is a quitter
like a two-legged stool –
it tries to stand
but it falls down.

He is like a trumpet –
it makes an awful noise.

So I give everyone a warning –
he is like chips,
he is not good for you.

6　Now read both poems again. Heather and Owen each created their poem by going through the same first stages as you now have. Can you work out what they have done with their list of notes to make them into a poem? Look at the last idea each of them has used. Why do you think Heather and Owen kept these particular ideas for their endings?

7　Heather and Owen have each taken a different approach. How many ideas has each of them used? How much has each of them said about each idea? How have they each structured their poem on the page?

8　Heather has used metaphor throughout her poem. Owen has used simile. What one word reveals the use of simile?

Now conduct the following experiment. Select a volunteer to read Heather's poem out loud but adding the word 'like' before each image. How does this change her poem? Is metaphor or simile more effective?

Now select a volunteer to read Owen's poem out loud but missing out the word 'like'. How does this change his poem? Again, is metaphor or simile more effective?

As a writer, you always have choices. If you know what your choices are, and you know what effect you are trying to achieve, then your writing will improve.

9   Now you are going to edit your own notes. First, you have to select the best, the most unusual, the funniest ideas you have come up with. Read over your notes again and put a star in the margin beside between four and eight of your favourite lines. If you are inspired with new ideas, you can add them in now too.

Next, before you rewrite them, decide what order you want to put them in. Keep the best for last. You might see a pattern emerging. If you do, use it.

10   Finally, on your second page of paper, write a first draft of your poem. You can use either Heather or Owen's poem as a model. You can still change words and add ideas, if you want. Finally, give it an original title. Well done!

This is a creative process that you can use over again. If you have written a poem about someone you dislike, you can now try writing one about someone you like. You can write a poem about someone you have lost from your life or you can write a poem about someone you have gained. Or you can write a poem about an animal.

Jim C. Wilson's Masterpiece

Spring

Arctic wind in May
comes cutting through blossom.
A soft pink blizzard.

Swifts screech past windows;
they've come from nowhere, sudden
as warmth on walls.

The stone-cold river
fills up with light; a dipper
skims on bits of sky.

Summer

An aeroplane hums
through the blue, as far away
as a child's summer.

Swallows swoop over
the old stone bridge that shadows
motionless trout.

Slow bees exploring
mouths of flowers; petals
quiver, poised to fall.

Autumn

Dry leaves like cracked tongues
hang in autumn smoke; the wind
tells bedtime stories.

Red berries hang bright,
replete with sun and summer;
soon they'll dry to seed.

The swifts have vanished;
the sun, burning low, shows us
another absence.

Winter

This year the first flake
of snow before the last leaf
of November falls.

In December hours
of darkness, a sudden star
through tangled branches.

Frozen fingers ache
around a rigid snowball.
Then the trickling thaw.

Questions

 ### Appreciating this masterpiece

Read Jim's poem once more before you go any further.

Jim has had fun making patterns here. Even before you read this poem, you can see the pattern on the page. (If you want to see the shape better, look at it again but with your eyes half-shut so that you can't read the actual words.)

There are four sections, each with the title of a season, and each section has three three-line verses.

If you look more closely, you will see that each 'verse' is a haiku. This is a seventeenth century Japanese poetry form, usually related to the seasons, with a maximum of 5–7–5 syllables (although there can be fewer) in each line. Rhyme is not used.

Look again at Spring. List as many ideas as you can that link back to winter, and that link forwards to summer.

In Summer, what emotion do you think Jim is trying to evoke with the simile 'as far away as a child's summer'? Why?

How does the sound in the first Summer haiku connect to the sound in the third Summer haiku?

Look at the second Summer haiku again. How has the river changed from the way it was in the third Spring haiku?

How does the third Summer haiku connect forwards to autumn?

What time of day has it become in Autumn? Why is this appropriate for this season? How many losses does Jim record here? How does the first line of the first autumn haiku connect to the third line? What kinds of bedtime stories do you think the wind tells?

In Winter, Jim has deliberately inverted the normal word order in the first haiku: where should the verb be? In light of the content of this haiku, why is this a masterly thing to do?

What time of day has it now become in the second Winter haiku? And how does this haiku connect back to the first Autumn haiku?

What does the star symbolise?

How does the third Winter haiku connect forwards to the following spring?

In addition to these fairly obvious patterns, there are subtler ones that Jim has also crafted.

This is a poem that recreates the continual movement from one season to the next. Go through the whole poem again and list all the things that move, or are about to move, through the air. The number may surprise you!

We have already seen how Jim uses the time of day to represent the seasons. Go through the poem again and look at his use of temperature, and colour, and sound.

This is a sensual poem, working on your eye and ear and sensations through the words and ideas that Jim has chosen.

But, in addition, Jim uses linguistic and poetic techniques. See if you can find examples of alliteration, onomatopoeia, internal rhyme and arresting line breaks.

Look again at the third Spring haiku. Explain the metaphorical use of language in the two images in the second and third lines. How effective do you think this is and why?

Three masterly techniques used by Jim

1 Handling a regular poetic form successfully.

2 Using the idea of movement and change as a cyclical thematic element. (This means that the idea behind the poem is of things like days or seasons or years coming round and round like enormous wheels made out of time. Look back at the section on Metaphor and Abstract Nouns (page 23) if this is difficult for you to understand.)

3 Exploiting the sound of language for poetic effect.

Your masterpiece

Jim, being a master of haiku, has written a series of linked haiku based on all four seasons. Normally, haiku are single three-line poems, complete in themselves, depicting a moment in time and in nature. The idea behind them is to empathise with the natural world and to see it with heightened senses.

The best place for inspiration is outside, although sometimes the natural world also finds its way inside!

Now try to write one (or more) of your own haiku. Here are some guidelines to help you.

1 Try to give yourself time to sink into the experience of connecting with the natural world, perhaps with a bird, an animal, a plant, the weather...

2 Try to observe it very closely with all your senses turned on, and think in visual images, sounds and perhaps smells.

3 See if you can use the idea of change or movement, and be aware of the cyclical nature of things.

4 Try to create a certain mood and to change the way we see ordinary things.

5 Individual haiku do not have titles.

6 Haiku do not rhyme.

7 Haiku are written in the present tense (check Jim's?) to make them more immediate.

8 Haiku can be written without capital letters or punctuation.

9 Haiku have three lines, each with no more than 5–7–5 syllables.

Here are some individual haiku to give you the idea. Read each slowly, twice.

> a spider-brown bead
> parachutes down the stairwell
> depending on silk

> a sliver of moon
> vicious as a kitten's claw
> scratches the twilight

> sparrow on a wire
> sunset burnishing its breast
> to passing bullfinch

> the white hare
> leaves white prints
> in snow

Each of these haiku is just a small moment of observation that tries to let you see a small part of the natural world in a different way.

Like many poems, the ideas are expressed in a very compact, compressed way. This is why we should read poems slowly. And several times. Their meaning is very concentrated.

For example, we could expand the spider haiku and say:

> A spider is coming down the stairwell on a line of web.
> The spider's legs are spread out and it is floating down as
> if it were a parachute. Also, the spider's web is a kind of
> silk and parachutes used to be made of silk.

Put like that, it's not really much of a haiku!

There is also a pun in the spider haiku on the word 'depending'
which means, literally, 'hanging from' and also, metaphorically,
'relying upon'.

Now try to write one or more of your own.

If you want to be more ambitious, see if you can write several linked
haiku.

You will find it easier if you choose a subject with some movement
or progression, in the same way as Jim chose the cycle of the four
seasons. This could be, for example, three stages in the life-cycle of
a butterfly or a frog.

You will find it easier if you give yourself some quiet time to think
and reflect on ideas. Ideas sometimes need to be encouraged. And
one idea will often lead to another, better idea. So give yourself
time, make notes and trust that you will find inspiration, or that
inspiration will find you. If not, creative writing is also about
travelling hopefully!

This is just a brief introduction to haiku for you. If you are
interested in learning more, there is a British Haiku Society. You can
find full details in the Appendix (page 166).

The Songs of Fish

Gordon Meade's Masterpiece

We all know the songs
Of whales and the sonar clicks

Of bottle-nosed dolphins.
We've heard them all

On our television sets.
But there are others

We haven't heard, and
Some we'd rather forget...

The damselfish's chirp
And the minnow's purr,

The cod's lone grunt
And the haddock's whirr,

The flounder's lullaby
And the sole's lament,

The trout's apology
And the grayling's complaint,

The eel's rattle
And the conger's shake,

The zander's death march
And the herring's wake,

The stickleback's ditty
And the witch's spell,

The lumpsucker's ragtime
And the spurdog's hell,

The thornback's skiffle
And the whiting's swing,

The barbel's ballad
And the mullet's din,

The plaice's anthem
And the roach's soul,

The bass's rock
And the dace's roll,

The carp's cool jazz
And the bleak's soft psalm,

The bream's blue grass
And the dab's alarm,

The mackerel's whistle
And the shark's dry laugh,

The salmon's swan-song
And the pike's last gasp.

Questions

 ## Appreciating this masterpiece

First, reread Gordon's poem, preferably aloud.

This masterly poem is about having fun with words, sounds and ideas. As far as you know, do any fish have voices with which they can sing? What is it that distinguishes whales and dolphins, who *can* produce sounds, from fish?

Like many other masterly writers in this book, Gordon has pushed an idea from reality into a more creative place. How much is this poem pushing reality? How true *could* it be?

Gordon uses the first person plural at the beginning of this poem. Can you explain the effect that this has on us, and why it is much better than first person singular?

Comment on the impact of the break between the end of the second verse and the start of the third verse. What is Gordon saying about the way in which we experience such sounds? How do you think he feels about this? Why?

What do you notice about the rhyming schemes here? Can you explain the differences in pattern by relating them to the content? Give two examples of perfect rhymes, and two examples of half rhymes. Try to explain the different impact that perfect rhyme and half rhyme has on us, and why.

Choose any three of the singing fish and suggest why Gordon has attributed that particular song to that particular fish.

Alliteration and onomatopoeia are important and appropriate in this poem about sound. Why is the last verse especially appropriate as the ending? (Find out what swansong means if you don't already know this.) Give three examples of especially effective use of sound and say why you think they are so good.

Comment also on the rhythm. How does the rhythm connect to the content?

What structural patterning can you see in the main part of this poem? What two lists has Gordon compiled to help him write this? In what kind of book could you find each list?

Look again at the main part of the poem, what pattern of repetition do you notice with both words and punctuation?

Look again at the verse about the eel and the conger. What other noisy eel-like creature is hidden there behind the words? Look at the last two words of each line, if you find this question confusing! This is a gift, a bonus connection, the kind of connection that happens when you're open to creative possibilities.

Can you find another verse where the last words in each line connect especially well to make a popular kind of music? What instrument used in this music is also suggested by one of the fish in this verse? And what place off the southeast coast of Scotland is suggested in the first line of that same verse? Why is this pun so appropriate given the subject of the poem?

Three masterly techniques used by Gordon

1 Drawing the reader in at the start.
2 Developing an unusual idea humorously.
3 Patterning with words, sounds and form.

Your masterpiece

Gordon's poem is both masterly and entertaining. Yet the structure is relatively simple and the process is, initially, mechanical.

Try your hand at your own pattern poem. You can't use fish or songs because they've both been done here, but you can think of your own pairings.

The 'creatures' could be different kinds of birds, dogs, cats, vehicles, weapons, sports...

The aspect about them could be different colours, different ways of moving, different noises (but not any of the fish's songs: there are plenty more noises), different places you'd find them, or any other ideas that suggest themselves to you.

Use reference books on your chosen subject to give you ideas and lists of words. You will also find a dictionary and a thesaurus helpful here.

Gordon's poem begins with reality, lifts into fantasy and resolves itself very satisfactorily at the end. See if you too can follow this pattern.

Enjoy this creative journey! Even if your resulting poem isn't as masterly as Gordon's, the process should be fun for you.

The Hawk

George Mackay Brown's Masterpiece

On Sunday the hawk fell on Bigging
    And a chicken screamed
    Lost in its own little snowstorm.
And on Monday he fell on the moor
    And the Field Club
    Raised a hundred silent prisms.
And on Tuesday he fell on the hill
    And the happy lamb
    Never knew why the loud collie straddled him.
And on Wednesday he fell on a bush
    And the blackbird
    Laid by his little flute for the last time.
And on Thursday he fell on Cleat
    And peerie Tom's rabbit
    Swung in a single arc from shore to hill.
And on Friday he fell on a ditch
    But the rampant rat,
    That eye and that tooth, quenched his flame.
And on Saturday he fell on Bigging
    And Jock lowered his gun
    And nailed a small wing over the corn.

Background information for you

George Mackay Brown was a writer who lived in the town of Stromness, on the Orkney Isles, which are off the north coast of Scotland. He was born in 1921 and died in 1996.

Bigging and Cleat are places on Orkney. See if you can research exactly where these two places are and how far apart they are.

The word 'bigging' is a Scots word for 'building' and 'peerie' is an Orcadian dialect word meaning 'small'. On the Shetland Isles, some 50 miles further north, their Shetlandic dialect word for 'small' is 'peedie'.

Questions

 Appreciating this masterpiece

First, make sure you understand what George is referring to when he writes of the Field Club's 'hundred silent prisms' and that you know the meaning of 'rampant'. (The root of this word can give you a clue.) One of the two flags of Scotland can also help you here with its image of a rampant creature. What is the creature, what position is it in and what image of Scots does this symbolise? How effective and appropriate to you think this image is?

Now, before going any further, read the poem again. Slowly.

As with several other poems in this book, this is a poem with a clear pattern.

George has written about a week in the life of a hawk, three lines for each day.

In as simple and clear English as you can, write the plain facts of what happens on each day. For example, 'on Monday the hawk caught a chicken'.

How successful a hunter is this hawk? The difference between your plain facts and how George transforms them by his creative expression is what writing poetry is all about. It is not so much *what* he says, as the *way* he says it.

George is a master of the poetic image giving us pictures and emotions. He deliberately uses unexpected words to make us stop and think and see things differently. For example, what words would you normally use for a hawk 'going for' its prey? George uses

'fell' seven times. How is the meaning of 'fell' changed the final time? Can you think of any other 'fields' of 'fallen'?

There are four deaths in this poem. How does George want us to feel about the first three victims?

On Saturday, at the end of the poem, in the last line, the Hawk is referred to simply as 'a small wing'. How does this contrast with the predator of the earlier days? How does George want us to feel about the hawk? And about Jock?

What happens on Sunday that Jock might try to use as justification for illegally killing a protected bird?

George knows the power of meaning and sound. We have seen how he uses unusual words, like the 'happy' lamb instead of 'lucky' lamb and the 'loud' collie instead of 'barking' collie. He also exploits imagery which gives us the pictures in our mind, and uses alliteration, vowel length and assonance to bring the music of poetry to our ears.

Comment on his metaphors for the death of the chicken on Monday and of the blackbird on Wednesday, and on his use of alliteration in both of these descriptions.

Look again at Thursday. What age do you think 'peerie Tom' is, whose rabbit the hawk takes? Look more closely at the line, '… Swung in a single arc from shore to hill.' Here, George uses long vowels and alliteration and assonance to connect the meaning with the movement. Give an example of two of those devices and say what effect you think they achieve.

Look at the way George deliberately repeats the word 'and' throughout the poem. What happens on Friday that breaks this pattern? What metaphor does George use for the hawk? How does 'ditch' connect with the idea of 'quench'?

Finally, in this poem about killing, how does the last word contain the promise of new life?

Three masterly techniques used by George

1 Making us see things differently by using unexpected words and images.

2 Enhancing the meaning by using linguistic sound effects.

3 Using a regular pattern with a twist at the end.

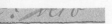

Your masterpiece

This is a challenging task and you will need to be able to concentrate, and to find stillness in your head into which your ideas will float. Take your time!

Think of a predator, domestic or wild. Think of two or three more predators. Never settle for your first idea, always dig deeper for greater originality.

Take a week in its life (its last week?).

Following George's pattern, make a list of seven daily encounters, in as plain and simple English as you want. Then, when you know what the content is, use your imagination and creative skills to express these events poetically with vocabulary, images and literary techniques like metaphor, simile, assonance, alliteration and internal rhyme to craft a poem that captures the spirit of both your predator and its prey.

Castle O Burrian

Yvonne Gray's Masterpiece

Puffins, windblown, come careering
in, wings a-tilt,
bright feet braced,
outstretched to catch
the ledge. They gather in rows
on narrow balconies,
tiny, gaudy, gossiping gods,
paintbox beaks a-gabble,
heads tweaking to this side
and that as they spotlight
what comings? what goings?
among guillemot groundlings
below. For now it's all
comedy, circus, spectacle,
the waves' drumthunder
an off-stage roll, the stormclouds
curtained back. The great black-backed's
cloak is folded:
its murderous eyes
look elsewhere.

Questions

 ## Appreciating this masterpiece

George Mackay Brown spent almost his whole life living in
Stromness on the Orkney Islands. Yvonne too lives there, and, like
George Mackay Brown's poem, her poem is set in the natural world
and also features birds.

Read Yvonne's poem again, preferably aloud.

Which two words in the first sentence do you think best capture the
erratic quality of a puffin's flight?

Comment on the impact of Yvonne's choice of line break at the end
of line 1 and line 4? What effect do the line breaks have? You might
like to think about rhythm and suspense. How does the start of line
2 affect the meaning of line 1, and the start of line 5 affect the
meaning of line 4? Comment on any other particularly effective
line breaks that you also notice.

Yvonne uses an extended metaphor, a theatrical one, in her poem.
Can you find four words that are more normally associated with an
indoor show? Who and what is the baddie, and how do you know
this? Why do you think he is such a threat?

Yvonne has also used sound effects in her poem. Can you find two
examples of each of the following: alliteration, assonance,
onomatopoeia, internal rhyme, and long and short vowels for
effect?

How do the last six lines of the poem change the tone from that of
the earlier lines?

What impression do you get of the character of the puffin? And
what kind of environment do puffins live in? What is the weather
like?

What kind of place do you think Castle O Burrian is? See if you can
find out *exactly* what and where it is. (You'll probably need to
research this!)

Three masterly techniques used by Yvonne

1 Devising an extended metaphor.
2 Creating sound effects using assonance, onomatopoeia,
 alliteration and internal rhyme.
3 Creating arresting line breaks.

Your masterpiece

Here are three ideas for you. The first one is a challenging one. The second and third are more straightforward.

Yvonne hasn't just glanced at a puffin or two and then written her poem. Can you sense the amount of quiet and motionless observation that she's made of these wild creatures? Can you also sense the time that she has set aside afterwards, in which to think about what she experienced with her eyes and her ears and her feelings? And the time needed to come up with a metaphor that can be extended through the whole poem?

This is what any serious writer has to do to create a poem or a story. Usually alone, and usually at a time of their own choosing.

She also has a writer's mind, which means you go through life with half an eye out for inspiration for a poem or a story. In the same way as photographers 'think in rectangles', writers think in ideas and images and connections.

You too can also encourage this creative state of mind. Try it. Look long and hard at something in your world. Inside or out. A flower? A spider's web? A roof line? A collection of DVDs?

Look for something else, either with your eyes or in your imagination, that connects to it in some way, that will set up some tension.

For example, a roof line with aerials, plus a distant plane... both are thin lines of metal... crosses?... memorials to missed programmes?... planes as flying aerials... carrying programmes, not passengers?... flights of fancy?... look for something else on the skyline for inspiration?... introduce a bird?... ariel/arial displays?... a storm bringing down aerials/birds/planes...

Just try it. Let your mind run free. Let unexpected connections and patterns emerge. Don't reject any ideas. Test them, see if they'll run. See if your ideas can be focused into a poem.

Even if you don't end up with a masterpiece, the process will be good for you. And you will be surprised at how many more ideas come along, given the chance. The more you do this, the more creative you will become.

Or:

Here is a second idea that you might find easier to do!

Write about an endangered species. See if you can explain why the
problem has arisen, and suggest possible solutions.

Or:

Write about your favourite wild place, describing the birds, plants,
animals, weather, landscape or seascape. See if you can capture the
moods of the place, using similes and metaphors, and any other
literary devices you want, to help you.

Voices O Quendale Bay

Christine De Luca's Masterpiece

The language and the context

Language

The following poem is written in the dialect of the Shetland Isles where Christine was born and brought up. Unless you're already familiar with Shetlandic, this poem might seem, at first glance, to be written in a completely foreign language.

However, Shetlandic is a mixture of standard English words (some with phonetic spellings to capture the Shetland accent), Scots words and Norn words. Norn was the language spoken many centuries ago in both Orkney and Shetland when the islands belonged to Norway and were ruled by the Vikings. Both groups of islands were given to Scotland in 1469. (See if you can find out why Norway had to give their islands to Scotland…)

After they became Scottish, Norn was discouraged and it died out as a spoken language about two hundred years ago. Many of the Norn words remain, though, and these are still found in the dialects of these islands.

(You might also like to think about the word 'Sutherland', the name of one of the most *northerly* parts of mainland Scotland. It means 'the land to the south', and was so named from the point of view of those who lived on these even more northerly isles.)

Context

Here is more information you might also need to help you place this poem in context.

The south mainland of Shetland is a narrow peninsula, about twenty-miles long and no more than five miles wide. Quendale Bay is on the southern tip of this peninsula.

Here, in January 1993, an oil tanker, the M V Braer, was blown onto rocks in severe gales and began leaking oil. The ferocious storms continued, the Braer broke up five days later and her cargo of oil spilled out, causing an environmental and ecological disaster.

85,000 tonnes (that's 94 *million* litres) of crude oil polluted the sea, the coastline, farmland and the air. Oil slicks spread more than 25 miles north, turning the white surf to dark brown foam and the heavy toxic smell of hydrocarbons travelled even further. The whole economy of Shetland was affected, with farmland, fish farms, and the sea all badly polluted.

Countless seabirds, fish, shellfish, seals and otters were also victims. It has been estimated that 32,000 birds died. Ironically, one poor otter became an indirect casualty of the oil spill when it was killed on the road by a Norwegian television crew who had come to film the disaster!

Fortunately, the ferocity of the storms that created the disaster in the first place, also helped to break up and disperse the oil afterwards. And the Braer's cargo was light crude oil, not heavy crude oil, which meant it was less contaminating. So, although the impact was nonetheless disastrous, it could have been many times worse.

Christine also refers to 'Ninian'. St Ninian was an early Christian missionary. There is a ruined mediaeval chapel dedicated to him on St Ninian's Isle, in Shetland. There, in 1958, a hoard of ornate Pictish silver, known as the St Ninian's Isle Treasure, was uncovered by a young Shetland boy on an archaelogical dig.

The Poem

Christine's Shetlandic poem responds to the Braer disaster by personifying three groups of victims: puffins (tammie nories), ewes (yowes) and otters (dratsies) and then concludes by personifying the sea itself.

There is a long vowel sound in this poem that we don't have in English. This is written 'ö' and can found be in Scandinavian languages, in German and also in French, where it's spelt 'eu'. Examples of this sound are, in German: öl, (which means oil), schön, möbel, and in French: deux, peu, bleu. Try to use this sound if you can when you read the poem or listen to it in your head.

Voices O Quendale Bay

The muttering	Da tröttel o da tammie nories	*puffins*
	You're weel wint	*well-acquainted*
	wi tammie nories:	
beaks	nebs foo o eels	
	you tink wis cloons.	*us*
	We mak you gaff?	*laugh*
	Luk wis i da een	*in the eyes*
	an see wis gowl.	*weep*
complaining	Da nyaarm o da yowes	*ewes*
Since before	Sin afore Ninian	
	wir lambs ir shampsed	*have chewed*
salt	saat tang an waar.	*tang, waar: seaweeds*
foreshore	Da ebb is shilpet.	*sour*
Ugh!	Gadge! Whitna waageng's	*aftertaste*
	i wir trots!	*throats*
moaning	Da oobin o da dratsies	*otters*
twirl	We tirl i da sea fur fun,	
	hunt sweet fish; skirl	*squeal, whirl*
	freedom roond creels.	
	Da tide is turned.	
	We'r elted noo	*sticky, dirty*
	an lick pooshin.	*poison*
	Da sang o da sea	
Take no heed!	Never leet! Never leet!	
I've	A'm danced an A'm flet,	*scolded*
drowned	smored yon grötti-barrel.	*stinking-barrel*
	I sal maet you;	*feed, give meat to*
curl comfortingly	cöllie aboot you	
	wi whitest froad.	*froth, surf*

Questions

 Appreciating this masterpiece

Read the poem again first. Try to read it aloud.

Christine's poem has a clear four-section pattern. In which person are the first three sections written? How does this change in the fourth? Why?

What is the tone of the first three sections? What does this then become in the fourth one? Why is the colour in the last line so important, literally and symbolically?

Explain both the literal and metaphorical meanings of 'the tide has turned' in the third section.

There are two poems in this book in which puffins/tammie nories are threatened – by natural predators in 'Castle O Burrian' and by an oil spill here. However, these two threats pale into insignificance compared to the much greater threat they, and other members of their food chain, are now facing. The sea can no longer 'maet' them. See if you can find out why not. What are the 'eels' referred to in section one? What has happened to them? Why? What can be done?

This is a poem that is meant to be heard, rather than read on the page. Christine uses the rich sounds of Shetlandic and exploits vowel length and onomatopoeia. Can you give three examples of onomatopoeia? And three examples of long vowels used for effect? Can you also find three examples of internal rhyme?

Can you explain how the theme of feeding and nourishment is used in each of the first three sections, and how this progresses to a slightly different idea in the last section?

Water, land and air are three elements that are important in this poem. Can you explain how each of the three groups of creatures here, the tammie nories, the yowes and the dratsies, connects with each of these three elements, and in what ways the oil pollution has affected them. (In Shetland, yowes live on the seashore and eat various kinds of seaweeds.)

Look again at Gordon Meade's poem on page 145. He too is writing about the sea. What are the different purposes of each of these writers? What similarities are there? How does each use sound/voices?

Let's look a little closer at dialect. In this poem, we have already seen that Christine uses standard English words (some with phonetic spellings so that we pronounce them differently with something more like a Shetland accent), Scots words (for example, 'shilpet' and 'skirl'), and Norn words. See if you can pick out six words in standard English, six English words that are spelt phonetically, and six Norn words. You might need a good dictionary to help you.

Can you see how these words from different sources all work together to create a rich dialect? And can you see (or hear) how some of the Norn words are not so different from English?

Unless you were familiar with Shetlandic, this poem would have looked incomprehensible at first sight. Have you now learned enough Shetlandic to read this poem with complete understanding? Well done! Studying languages and dialects, their origins and their current use, can be fascinating, rewarding and good fun.

Three masterly techniques used by Christine

1 Writing in dialect with appropriate spelling and vocabulary.
2 Responding poetically to an environmental issue.
3 Giving us a strong sense of place.

Your masterpiece

Think of an environmental issue that concerns you. It might be sound or light pollution, or traffic fumes, or road-building, house-building, wind farms, pylons, fish farms, flooding or anything else.

See if you can think of four things that are affected for better or for worse. You might find it helpful to think of three that are badly affected and one that benefits, or vice versa. This could help you to set up your ending.

Now try to personify them, giving them voices in the same way as Christine has done. They could be critical or complaining voices or celebrating.

Work out a regular pattern for your poem so that it looks pleasing on the page.

Think about the sound as well as the meaning of your words.

Try to use onomatopoeia, alliteration and internal rhyme.

And if you want any of your voices to speak in dialect, here's your chance!

Or:

Write a personal opinion piece on an environmental issue or animal rights issue that you feel strongly about. Try to structure it sensibly, explaining what the issue is, what its supporters say, what its critics say, what your own thoughts are and why.

APPENDIX

Acknowledgements

First, I would like to thank everyone, young and old, whose company and writing I have enjoyed in creative writing workshops over the last 20 years.

In particular, I would like to thank Martine Marletta and Bernadette MacPherson for enabling me to work with many young writers through the visionary Out of School Learning project run by Renfrewshire Libraries over the last three years. I would also like to thank Steve Cook, Education Officer of the Royal Literary Fund, for awarding me a Writing Fellowship to work with teachers, both in training and in service.

For their expert help with aspects of Part One, The Writer's Toolkit, I would like to thank Professor Christian Kay of the Department of English Language at Glasgow University and Professor Jim McGonigal of the Department of Curriculum Studies, also at Glasgow University. Also, Duncan Jones, of the Association for Scottish Literary Studies, who has been invaluable for his help with several of the texts in Part Three, Masterpieces.

In addition, I would like to thank Franzesca Ewart and Dr Freda Hughes for help with research; Meredith Copland and Jan Culik for help with Czech pronunciation; Christine De Luca for help with all matters Shetlandic; and John Mitchell, Katherine Bennett and Elizabeth Hayes of Hodder Gibson for much help in putting this all together. Also Davina Baird and Nan Clowes for helping me to trace Kathleen Daly (whose recent death, at the age of 87, we now mourn), and last, but not least, Donald Beveridge for chocolate, and other sustenance, throughout the preparation and writing of this book.

Valerie Thornton

The Photographs

These photographs are found in between each masterpiece.

1 This enormous balanced rock can be found on the side of Ben Hogh on the island of Coll. There are other balanced rocks on the island too. No-one knows how they came to be balanced, nor when, nor whether they are natural or man-made.

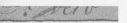

2   Shona the sheep was also found on Coll in the summer of 2003.

3   The furnished bus shelter was a surprise find on the Shetland Islands in 1996.

4   This young gannet was found washed up in the shallows on Feall Bay, on Coll, waterlogged, and badly entangled in blue nylon fishing line. I caught it, cut it free and carried it to dry on the rocks in the sunshine. I hope it survived: there was no body in evidence the next day.

5   Bumble, aged 18, in her half of a tenor saxophone case.

6   This amazing natural arch is called the Dore Holm and can be found off the coast of Esha Ness on the North Mainland of Shetland. In time, the narrow neck will be completely weathered away, resulting in two separate rock masses.

7   This skilfully-knotted fishing float was washed up on a beach on the Western Isles.

8   This tern chick was 'hiding', depending on its camouflage, on the island of Tiree, in June 2001.

9   The Meadowside Granary, Glasgow, in the process of demolition, summer 2003. The words had been 'Clyde Port Authority'. Shades of Ozymandias.

10   Sheep bone with snails, Coll, July 2004.

11   Alistair Hughes, exuberant in Alva, summer 2004.

12   Graffiti under the Clydeside Expressway, Partick, Glasgow, December 2003.

13   Ruin at the former graving docks, Kinning Park, Glasgow, winter 2000.

14   Former shop sign (bargain books) at the junction of Byres Road and White Street, Glasgow, summer 2003.

LILT

LILT (Language Into Languages Teaching) is a staff development resource for Scottish primary and secondary schools; however, it is also very helpful for pupils too. Funded by the Scottish Executive Education Department and produced by the University of Glasgow, it refreshes knowledge of grammar and linguistic concepts, and brings Knowledge about Language more confidently to the fore in schools.

A hard copy of the LILT pack (three booklets and a CD ROM) was issued to every school in Scotland. However, the entire package is now also available online:
http://www.arts.gla.ac.uk/SESLL/EngLang/LILT/frameset.htm

Scottish Short Story and Poetry Publications

Much good writing can be found in *New Writing Scotland*, an annual anthology since 1983 of poetry and short stories, published by the Association for Scottish Literary Studies (ASLS). ASLS is an organisation that supports the teaching, study, writing and reading of Scottish literature and language, past and present. Four of the masterpieces here, 'My Last Day at School', 'An Ignorance of Sound', 'The Songs of Fish' and 'Castle O Burrian', were first published in various issues of *New Writing Scotland*. It is free, annually, to members of ASLS, but it can also be purchased in bookshops. Contact Duncan Jones, ASLS, c/o Department of Scottish History, University of Glasgow, 9 University Gardens, Glasgow G12 8QH, telephone 0141 330 5309, email office@asls.org.uk or visit their website www.arts.gla.ac.uk/ScotLit/ASLS

Another source of good writing is 'Chapman' magazine. This literary magazine has been produced for more than 30 years. (Number 94 has another great story by Carolyn Mack, 'Learning to Read'.) You can contact them at Chapman, 4 Broughton Place, Edinburgh EH1 3RX, telephone 0131 557 2207, email chapman-pub@blueyonder.co.uk or visit their website at www.chapman-pub.co.uk

Helpful Organisations

The Scottish Poetry Library has an extremely knowledgeable and helpful staff, and thousands of poetry books. Further writing by most of the poets featured in Part Three of this book can be found there. Many of the library's books are also available on free postal loan to teachers, student teachers and school librarians anywhere in Scotland. The Scottish Poetry Library is at 5 Crichton's Close, Canongate, Edinburgh EH8 8DP, telephone 0131 557 2876, email education@spl.org.uk or visit their website at www.spl.org.uk

The Scottish Book Trust is Scotland's national agency for promoting reading, writing and books. Their Live Literature Scheme part-funds writers' visits to schools and contains a database of available writers which includes several of the writers featured in Part Three of this book. You can contact the Scottish Book Trust at Sandeman House, Trunk's Close, 55 High Street, Edinburgh EH1 1SR, telephone 0131 524 0160 email info@scottishbooktrust.com or visit their website at www.scottishbooktrust.com

The Pushkin Prizes encourages creative writing in children by running an annual competition, through schools, for S1 and S2 pupils in Scotland and St Petersburg, Russia. Extracts from writing by three Pushkin Prizewinners ('Determination', 'The Challenge' and 'A Midwinter Night's Dream') appear in Part Two of this book. These stories were first published in full in the excellent Pushkin Prizes' annual anthologies. Contact the Pushkin Prizes, c/o Fraser Ross Associates, 6 Wellington Place, Edinburgh, EH6 7EQ. 0131 553 2759 or email lindsey.fraser@tiscali.co.uk or visit their website at www.pushkinprizes.net

The British Haiku Society promotes the writing and teaching of haiku and produces an excellent (and very reasonably-priced) Haiku Kit teaching pack. Visit their website at www.haikusoc.ndo.co.uk/first.html for more information.